"This series is a tremendous resource for those w: understanding of how the gospel is woven throu᷄ pastors and scholars doing gospel business from all the Scriptures. This is a biblical and theological feast preparing God's people to apply the entire Bible to all of life with heart and mind wholly committed to Christ's priorities."

> **BRYAN CHAPELL,** President Emeritus, Covenant Theological Seminary; Senior Pastor, Grace Presbyterian Church, Peoria, Illinois

"Mark Twain may have smiled when he wrote to a friend, 'I didn't have time to write you a short letter, so I wrote you a long letter.' But the truth of Twain's remark remains serious and universal, because well-reasoned, compact writing requires extra time and extra hard work. And this is what we have in the Crossway Bible study series *Knowing the Bible*. The skilled authors and notable editors provide the contours of each book of the Bible as well as the grand theological themes that bind them together as one Book. Here, in a 12-week format, are carefully wrought studies that will ignite the mind and the heart."

> **R. KENT HUGHES,** Visiting Professor of Practical Theology, Westminster Theological Seminary

"*Knowing the Bible* brings together a gifted team of Bible teachers to produce a high-quality series of study guides. The coordinated focus of these materials is unique: biblical content, provocative questions, systematic theology, practical application, and the gospel story of God's grace presented all the way through Scripture."

> **PHILIP G. RYKEN,** President, Wheaton College

"These *Knowing the Bible* volumes provide a significant and very welcome variation on the general run of inductive Bible studies. This series provides substantial instruction, as well as teaching through the very questions that are asked. *Knowing the Bible* then goes even further by showing how any given text links with the gospel, the whole Bible, and the formation of theology. I heartily endorse this orientation of individual books to the whole Bible and the gospel, and I applaud the demonstration that sound theology was not something invented later by Christians, but is right there in the pages of Scripture."

> **GRAEME L. GOLDSWORTHY,** former lecturer, Moore Theological College; author, *According to Plan, Gospel and Kingdom, The Gospel in Revelation,* and *Gospel and Wisdom*

"What a gift to earnest, Bible-loving, Bible-searching believers! The organization and structure of the Bible study format presented through the *Knowing the Bible* series is so well conceived. Students of the Word are led to understand the content of passages through perceptive, guided questions, and they are given rich insights and application all along the way in the brief but illuminating sections that conclude each study. What potential growth in depth and breadth of understanding these studies offer! One can only pray that vast numbers of believers will discover more of God and the beauty of his Word through these rich studies."

> **BRUCE A. WARE,** Professor of Christian Theology, The Southern Baptist Theological Seminary

KNOWING THE BIBLE

J. I. Packer, Theological Editor
Dane C. Ortlund, Series Editor
Lane T. Dennis, Executive Editor

•　　　•　　　•　　　•　　　•　　　•

Genesis	Psalms	Jonah, Micah, and Nahum	Ephesians
Exodus	Proverbs		Philippians
Leviticus	Ecclesiastes	Haggai, Zechariah, and Malachi	Colossians and Philemon
Numbers	Song of Solomon		
Deuteronomy	Isaiah	Matthew	1–2 Thessalonians
Joshua	Jeremiah	Mark	1–2 Timothy and Titus
Judges	Lamentations, Habakkuk, and Zephaniah	Luke	
Ruth and Esther		John	Hebrews
1–2 Samuel	Ezekiel	Acts	James
1–2 Kings	Daniel	Romans	1–2 Peter and Jude
1–2 Chronicles	Hosea	1 Corinthians	1–3 John
Ezra and Nehemiah	Joel, Amos, and Obadiah	2 Corinthians	Revelation
Job		Galatians	

•　　　•　　　•　　　•　　　•　　　•

J. I. PACKER was the former Board of Governors' Professor of Theology at Regent College (Vancouver, BC). Dr. Packer earned his DPhil at the University of Oxford. He is known and loved worldwide as the author of the best-selling book *Knowing God*, as well as many other titles on theology and the Christian life. He served as the General Editor of the ESV Bible and as the Theological Editor for the *ESV Study Bible*.

LANE T. DENNIS is CEO of Crossway, a not-for-profit publishing ministry. Dr. Dennis earned his PhD from Northwestern University. He is Chair of the ESV Bible Translation Oversight Committee and Executive Editor of the *ESV Study Bible*.

DANE C. ORTLUND (PhD, Wheaton College) serves as senior pastor of Naperville Presbyterian Church in Naperville, Illinois. He is an editor for the Knowing the Bible series and the Short Studies in Biblical Theology series, and is the author of several books, including *Gentle and Lowly: The Heart of Christ for Sinners and Sufferers*.

RUTH AND ESTHER

A 12-WEEK STUDY

Kathleen B. Nielson

:: CROSSWAY®

WHEATON, ILLINOIS

Published by Crossway
           1300 Crescent Street
           Wheaton, Illinois 60187

Cover design: Simplicated Studio

First printing 2014

Printed in the United States of America

Trade paperback ISBN: 978-1-4335-4038-7
ePub ISBN: 978-1-4335-4041-7
PDF ISBN: 978-1-4335-4039-4
Mobipocket ISBN: 978-1-4335-4040-0

Crossway is a publishing ministry of Good News Publishers.

VP			31	30	29	28	27	26	25	24	23
20	19	18	17	16	15	14	13	12	11	10	

TABLE OF CONTENTS

SERIES PREFACE

KNOWING THE BIBLE, as the series title indicates, was created to help readers know and understand the meaning, the message, and the God of the Bible. Each volume in the series consists of 12 units that progressively take the reader through a clear, concise study of that book of the Bible. In this way, any given volume can fruitfully be used in a 12-week format either in group study, such as in a church-based context, or in individual study. Of course, these 12 studies could be completed in fewer or more than 12 weeks, as convenient, depending on the context in which they are used.

Each study unit gives an overview of the text at hand before digging into it with a series of questions for reflection or discussion. The unit then concludes by highlighting the gospel of grace in each passage ("Gospel Glimpses"), identifying whole-Bible themes that occur in the passage ("Whole-Bible Connections"), and pinpointing Christian doctrines that are affirmed in the passage ("Theological Soundings").

The final component to each unit is a section for reflecting on personal and practical implications from the passage at hand. The layout provides space for recording responses to the questions proposed, and we think readers need to do this to get the full benefit of the exercise. The series also includes definitions of key words. These definitions are indicated by a note number in the text and are found at the end of each chapter.

Lastly, to help understand the Bible in this deeper way, we urge readers to use the ESV Bible and the *ESV Study Bible*, which are available in various print and digital formats, including online editions at esv.org. The Knowing the Bible series is also available online.

May the Lord greatly bless your study as you seek to know him through knowing his Word.

J. I. Packer
Lane T. Dennis

WEEK 1: OVERVIEW OF RUTH

Getting Acquainted

Two books in the Bible are named after women: Ruth and Esther. These women lived approximately five centuries apart, one in the period leading up to the kingdom of Israel,[1] and the other following the kingdom's decline and fall. One was a foreigner who came to the land of Judah; the other was a Jew who lived in a foreign land. God has always been at work in the whole world he made and over which he rules. Both women played crucial roles in the big story of God's redeeming[2] a people for himself from all the nations through his Son.

We begin with Ruth, a foreigner who found a home in Bethlehem. She lived during the period of the judges, when there was yet no king in Israel and "everyone did what was right in his own eyes" (Judg. 21:25). This masterful narrative is about Ruth, but it is even more about God's covenant[3] kindness to his people—even in the midst of their repeated rebellion against him. Ruth's mother-in-law, Naomi, doubts but then learns this kindness, as Ruth and Boaz live it out before her eyes. In four artfully shaped scenes, these three characters live *the story of a God who provides for his people according to his promises.*

The narrative draws us into the experience of these widowed women who move from empty desolation in Moab to full provision back in Bethlehem. But the story keeps lifting our eyes in the process, letting us glimpse the God in charge of famine and harvest and barrenness and birth and death and indeed every scene of human history. Reading the book of Ruth, we marvel at Ruth's story and we see more clearly the God who so kindly directs it. (For further background, see the *ESV Study Bible*, pages 475–477, or visit esv.org.)

Placing It in the Larger Story

God's covenant promises to Abraham (Gen. 12:1–7) are beautifully displayed in Ruth. Although the period in which she lived was one of disobedience and disarray, God had indeed made Abraham's seed into a great people and settled them in the Land of Promise. In Ruth's life, the blessing[4] promised to those who bless God's people proves true. As she, the foreigner, is enfolded among them, we catch a glimpse of all the families of the earth being blessed by Abraham's seed.

The crowning evidence of God's covenant faithfulness emerges at the book's end, with the repeated mention of Ruth's descendant David (Ruth 4:17–22), the great king to whom God promised an eternal throne (2 Sam. 7:12–17). But this blessing peeks through from the moment we open Ruth and begin to read about Bethlehem in Judah—Judah being the land named after the tribe from which David came. The Scriptures ultimately show the fulfillment of all God's promises in the coming of Jesus Christ, the heavenly king born in Bethlehem, in the line of David. Matthew 1:1–6 gives us the genealogy that Ruth helps unfold in living color.

The book of Ruth is one episode in the story of Jesus. It's an episode that shows the utterly magnificent and intensely personal kindness of this God who is redeeming a people for himself from all the families of the earth. As God fulfills all Ruth's and Naomi's needs for food, home, and family, through their redeemer Boaz, we glimpse the heavenly Redeemer in whom all these needs are finally and fully met.

Key Verse

"Then the women said to Naomi, 'Blessed be the LORD, who has not left you this day without a redeemer, and may his name be renowned in Israel!'" (Ruth 4:14).

Date and Historical Background

Ruth's story takes place "in the days when the judges ruled" (Ruth 1:1). The book of Judges describes this period (c. 13th–11th centuries BC) as a downward-spiraling cycle of sinful[5] rebellion by God's people, followed by cries for help to God who sends a deliverer/judge, followed again by sinful rebellion. Such a background for Ruth's story highlights both the need for and the wonder of God's merciful[6] faithfulness to his people.

The book's concluding genealogy, with its mention of David, implies that it was composed later, after David's taking the throne in c. 1010 BC.

Outline

   I. Introduction: Naomi Bereft of Family (1:1–5)

  II. Scene 1: Naomi Returns to Bethlehem with Ruth (1:6–22)

 III. Scene 2: Ruth Gleans in Boaz's Field (2:1–23)

 IV. Scene 3: Ruth, at the Threshing Floor, Asks Boaz to Marry Her (3:1–18)

  V. Scene 4: Boaz Arranges Redemption at the Gate (4:1–12)

 VI. Conclusion: Naomi Blessed with a New Family (4:13–17)

VII. Genealogy: Extended Blessing (4:18–22)

As You Get Started . . .

Do a quick read-through of Ruth, as if you were reading a short story. What aspects of the book stand out after such a reading? Jot down some of your initial observations.

This book called "Ruth" doesn't start and end with Ruth! Look at the prominent role of Naomi in the beginning (ch. 1) and the end (4:13–17). What do you notice? What are your thoughts at this point on why Naomi provides the "bookends" to this story?

On first reading, what specific words (perhaps repeated ones) or phrases stand out to you? Write them down. How might those words help clarify the big picture of what this book is about?

> ### As You Finish This Unit . . .

Take a moment now to ask God to bless you with increased understanding and a transformed heart and life as you study the book of Ruth. Look back through this introductory chapter and underline words or thoughts you would like to pray about or consider further. May the Spirit who inspired Scripture's living and active words use them to challenge and encourage our hearts.

Definitions

[1] **Israel** – Originally, another name given to Jacob (Gen. 32:28). Later applied to the nation formed by his descendants, then to the 10 northern tribes of that nation, who rejected the anointed king and formed their own nation. In the NT, the name is applied to the church as the spiritual descendants of Abraham (Gal. 6:16).

[2] **Redemption** – In the context of the Bible, the act of buying back someone who had become enslaved or something that had been lost to someone else. Through his death and resurrection, Jesus purchased redemption for all believers (Col. 1:13–14).

[3] **Covenant** – A binding agreement between two parties, typically involving a formal statement of their relationship, a list of stipulations and obligations for both parties, a list of witnesses to the agreement, and a list of curses for unfaithfulness and blessings for faithfulness to the agreement. God throughout Old Testament times established covenants with his people, all of which come to God's people finally through Christ, who inaugurated the new covenant (1 Cor. 11:25).

[4] **Bless** – To worship or praise another, especially God; to bestow goodness on another.

[5] **Sin** – Any violation of or failure to adhere to the commands of God.

[6] **Mercy** – Compassion and kindness toward someone experiencing hardship, sometimes even when such suffering results from the person's own sin or foolishness. God displays mercy toward his people and they, in turn, are called to display mercy toward others (Luke 6:36).

Week 2: Returning to Bethlehem

Ruth 1

The Place of the Passage

Ruth begins with a brief introduction and a dramatic first scene that set the stage for the whole narrative. In the midst of a desolate context both historically and personally, Naomi decides to return from Moab to Bethlehem. That return precipitates the action of the rest of the story, beginning immediately with Ruth's response. This chapter shows Naomi's emptiness in Moab which, by book's end, will turn into the fullness of God's provision in Bethlehem.

The Big Picture

Ruth 1 shows the context of Naomi's desolation (the time of the judges, famine, alienation from home, death, bitterness) and yet the seeds of hope in a return to a food-filled Bethlehem along with a faith-filled[1] daughter-in-law, Ruth.

> ### Reflection and Discussion

Read Ruth 1 slowly and carefully. Then consider and write your reflections on the following questions, which move through the chapter section by section. (For further background, see the *ESV Study Bible*, pages 478–479, or visit esv.org.)

1. Introduction: The Desolate Context (1:1–5)

For a glimpse into the period of the judges (1:1), read Judges 2:6–23 and 21:25. Why might this background be important for understanding the book of Ruth?

Elimelech evidently didn't intend to leave permanently the Land of Promise or his own particular clan, city, and tribe within it (1:2). He meant only to "sojourn" (1:1), or to *stay a while* in Moab, to escape the famine in Israel. Look on a map to find the land of Moab across the Dead Sea from Bethlehem. Moab's inhabitants were the descendants of an incestuous union between Lot and one of his daughters (Gen. 19:30–38). The Moabites worshiped other gods and were not friends of God's people (see Numbers 22–25). The story does not directly judge Elimelech, but in what ways might we see his move to Moab as problematic?

2. Naomi's Plan and Ruth's Determination (1:6–18)

The book's introduction leaves Naomi in crisis, with sons and husband dead (1:5). In that place and time, a woman without a man was without means of support, helpless and vulnerable. And a wife without children to continue the family line was regarded as a failure. Jewish law provided for "levirate marriage" (after the Latin *levir*, meaning "brother-in-law"), in which a brother was obliged to marry a childless widow of his deceased brother and to raise children in the brother's name (see Deut. 25:5–10). Naomi refers to this law as she addresses her two daughters-in-law. Observe and listen carefully to Naomi in Ruth 1:6–15, and make a list of everything you can discern about her.

Orpah took the sensible route and went home, but Ruth "clung" to her mother-in-law (v. 14). The same Hebrew word *dabaq* in Genesis 2:24 describes a man leaving his father and mother and "holding fast" to his wife. It's a strong word. Ruth's own words are strong and beautiful, full of poetic parallelism.[2] Make an outline of her statements (vv. 16–17). How do these statements grow, reaching a climax at the end? What do we learn here about Ruth?

3. The Return (1:19–22)

"Naomi" means "pleasant," but "Mara" means "bitter"—a name with which Naomi identifies at this point. In what ways does Naomi specifically attribute her bitterness to God in Ruth 1:13, 19–22? How might you evaluate her theology at this point?

Chapter 1 is dark with Naomi's bitterness. But what elements of hope can you observe throughout this chapter?

Dialogue is the main "meat" of each scene in this narrative. Ruth has the most powerful lines in chapter 1, but Naomi has the most! In what ways is it important and good for us to hear Naomi's words of bitter lament, acknowledged so fully in God's Word, here at this story's start?

Note the "return from the country of Moab" in both verse 6 and verse 22—providing bookends for this dramatic scene. The final verse repeatedly emphasizes *return*, for both Naomi and "Ruth the Moabite." This clearly represents a turning point in the story and in the experience of these women. Why is this return so important? How would you express what it is Naomi and Ruth are returning to? (For further context, read Josh. 1:1–6.)

We have described this book as *the story of a God who provides for his people according to his promises*. In what ways does chapter 1 lead us to begin considering the various parts of this description?

Read through the following three sections on *Gospel Glimpses, Whole-Bible Connections,* and *Theological Soundings.* Then take time to consider the *Personal Implications* these sections may have for you.

Gospel Glimpses

A HEART CHANGED BY GRACE.[3] We meet Ruth in this opening chapter only through words and actions, not through any narrative interpretation. But what we see strongly suggests a regenerative[4] work of God in Ruth, so that she gives her heart and her life not only to her mother-in-law but also to her mother-in-law's God. She has been drawn into a family that is part of God's people, where she clearly has heard enough about God to call him "LORD" (see "Whole-Bible Connections" below) and to begin to grasp the connection between God and his called-out people. Her words might even echo God's covenantal language to Abraham and his descendants, promising that he will be their God and they will be his people (see, for example, Gen. 17:7–8; Ex. 6:7). Such a story, like Rahab's before her (Joshua 2), makes us ask how and why God plucked this one person out of an ungodly nation. Why not Orpah? The text does not answer those questions but leaves us increasingly in awe of God's inexplicable grace that calls out sinners from every nation.

A RETURN. This chapter keeps reminding us that we are reading about a *return.* The gospel is all about God's providing a way for lost people to return to God— ever since Adam and Eve were separated from God by their sin but received his promise to provide a way for that sin to be defeated, through the seed (or "offspring") of the woman (Gen. 3:15). The shape of a *return story* resonates with the shape of redemption. The prophets called out again and again, "Return!" (see, for example, Hos. 14:1; Mal. 3:7). But they didn't simply call for a return. They pointed ahead to the means for that return: the promised Seed, the Lord and Savior Jesus Christ—the one born in Bethlehem, the very city to which Naomi is returning, in the land of God's promise. Scripture resounds with the call to return, ultimately to God himself. Both Naomi and Ruth follow this call and duly find the provision of God's grace.

Whole-Bible Connections

A COVENANT PEOPLE. God's promises to Abraham (Gen. 12:1–7) stand out as context for this story. The details of Elimelech's background (Ruth 1:2) establish that we're dealing with the sons of Jacob descended from Abraham who were divided into tribes—now numerous, as God promised, and settled in the land God promised. Accordingly, we feel the jarring of one of these descendants leaving the land; this jarring adds to the import of the *return*. We also feel the huge significance of a foreigner like Ruth so boldly purposing to become part of the people God has covenanted to bless. Only as the story develops do we with fuller understanding celebrate the way Ruth's enfolding into Israel is actually a beautiful part of the fulfillment of God's promise to Abraham that, in him, "all the families of the earth shall be blessed" (Gen. 12:3).

HESED. Ruth 1:8 brings the first of several appearances in this book of a profoundly beautiful Old Testament Hebrew word, *hesed*, often translated "steadfast love," "loving kindness," or simply "kindness." *Hesed* can refer both to human kindness and, in many instances, to the loving kindness of God toward his people. When God in his glory passes by Moses hidden in the cleft of the rock, there in Exodus 34:6 shines God's "steadfast love," surrounded by his mercy and faithfulness, and poured out on generations of his people. The Psalms repeatedly celebrate God's *hesed* (see, for example, Ps. 103:4; 106:7; Psalm 136). When we come upon it in Ruth 1:8, this word shines out, especially as it connects with the Lord's own kindness—offered in blessing by one of Abraham's descendants (Naomi) but referring to kindness passed on by those not in Abraham's line (Naomi's daughters-in-law). We shall see this word again in Ruth.

YAHWEH. When commissioned by God to lead his people out of Egypt, Moses asked God how to answer concerning the name of the one who had sent him. "God said to Moses, 'I AM WHO I AM.' And he said, 'Say this to the people of Israel, "I AM has sent me to you"'" (Ex. 3:14). God here reveals his name "Yahweh" (corresponding to the four Hebrew consonants *YHWH*), which expresses both God's eternal being and his unfailing love for his people to whom he reveals himself. It is not surprising that Naomi, an Israelite, repeatedly uses this name, indicated in the English text by "LORD." However, Ruth's use of this name stands out. In her speech, Ruth first refers to Naomi's "God," with the more universally understood name (1:16). But in her climactic statement she implies a relationship between this God and herself, referring to him as "LORD," or "Yahweh" (v. 17). This seems a large hint that God has shown Ruth his *hesed*, as she has learned of him, taken this *hesed* to heart, and let it flow through her to those around.

Theological Soundings

PROVIDENCE.[5] God's providence hovers over this chapter. The initial mention of famine brings to mind God's control over nature and use of it for his purposes (see, for example, Gen. 42:5 and Deut. 11:13–14). Naomi does not hear just that the famine is over in Israel but also that "the LORD had visited his people and given them food" (1:6). "Food" here means literally "bread"— as in "Bethlehem," which means literally "house of bread." God is clearly at work, providing, *visiting* his people in substantial ways. We recall Joseph, who in God's providence provided grain for his family and for all of famine-struck Egypt (Gen. 45:4–11), and who as he was dying prophesied God's visitation to his people that would come in the exodus (50:24–25). One might think of Zechariah's prophecy concerning the baby to be born in Bethlehem: "Blessed be the Lord God of Israel, for he has visited and redeemed his people" (Luke 1:68). When Ruth 1 ends with the mention of barley harvest in Bethlehem, we sense God's providential hand at work and look forward to seeing his provision on many levels.

SOVEREIGNTY.[6] God is in charge of this history, and Naomi knows it. She does not envision herself at the mercy of a random or chaotic universe. Even though she misunderstands God's kind purposes, she does understand that a sovereign "Almighty" has brought about everything that has happened to her (1:20, 21). Naomi knows the Lord God Almighty rules, and she will learn to acknowledge his kindness even along the painful path on which he leads her.

Personal Implications

Take time to reflect on the implications of Ruth 1 for your own life today. Make notes below on the personal implications for your walk with the Lord that you find in the (1) *Gospel Glimpses*, (2) *Whole-Bible Connections*, (3) *Theological Soundings*, and (4) this passage as a whole.

1. Gospel Glimpses

2. Whole-Bible Connections

3. Theological Soundings

4. Ruth 1

As You Finish This Unit . . .

Take a moment now to ask for the Lord's blessing and help as you continue in this study of Ruth. Take a moment also to look back through this unit of study, to reflect on a few key things that the Lord may be teaching you—and perhaps to highlight and underline these things to review again in the future.

Definitions

[1] **Faith** – Trust in or reliance upon something or someone despite a lack of concrete proof. Here the "someone" is God. Salvation, which is purely a work of God's grace, can be received only through faith (Rom. 5:2; Eph. 2:8–9). The writer of Hebrews calls on believers to emulate those who lived godly lives by faith (Hebrews 11).

[2] **Parallelism** – A poetic device, employed in virtually all Hebrew poetry, that places together two or three concepts that are matching, opposing, or progressive in meaning. Essentially it is a "rhyming" of concepts rather than of sounds.

[3] **Grace** – Unmerited favor, especially the free gift of salvation that God gives to believers through faith in Jesus Christ.

[4] **Regeneration** – The Holy Spirit's work of bringing spiritual life to a person, thus enabling him or her to love and follow God. Essentially equivalent to what is often referred to as being "born again" or "saved."

[5] **Providence** – God's good, wise, and sovereign guidance and control of all things, by which he supplies all our needs and accomplishes his holy will.

[6] **Sovereignty** – Supreme and independent power and authority. Sovereignty over all things is a distinctive attribute of God (1 Tim. 6:15–16). He directs all things to carry out his purposes (Rom. 8:28–29).

Week 3: A Meeting in the Barley Field

Ruth 2

▲

The Place of the Passage

After Naomi's "empty" return to Bethlehem along with Ruth, we are ready to see how God will fill her. Scene two begins to unfold God's full provision for these women, as Ruth goes out to glean and encounters Boaz. The scene overflows with God's kind, abundant provision through Boaz, and it sets up the expectation of seeing how this encounter of Ruth and Boaz might develop.

The Big Picture

God's kindness is demonstrated and recognized as Ruth leaves Naomi to glean, finds herself welcomed and abundantly provided for in Boaz's field, and then returns to tell Naomi all about this gracious provision.

> ### Reflection and Discussion

Read Ruth 2 slowly and carefully. Then consider and write your reflections on the following questions, which move through the chapter section by section. (For further background, see the *ESV Study Bible*, pages 479–481, or visit esv.org.)

1. Setting Up Boaz and Ruth (2:1–7)

Consider the ways in which the narrator introduces us to Boaz in the first four verses. Why this order of information, and what things can we discern about this man?

Jewish law made provision for the poor, sojourners, widows, and orphans to gather ("glean") grain that was standing in corners or borders of fields or that was dropped by reapers as they cut and tied the grain in sheaves (Lev. 19:9–10; 23:22; Deut. 24:19). Ruth qualifies for these gleanings in more than one category! As we watch her in verses 1–7, what things does the narrator want us to observe or discern about this young woman?

2. The Meeting of Boaz and Ruth (2:8–16)

What details of Boaz's abundant kindness to Ruth do you notice in Ruth 2:8–9, 14–16? What details do you enjoy, as they help you picture the scene?

Verses 10–13 give us the heart of this meeting, in the characters' words. First, what do Ruth's words show about her heart, in verse 10 and verse 13?

Boaz's words in verses 11–12 capture the essence of this conversation and of this chapter. As Boaz blesses Ruth with his words, he builds up to the most important thing she has done. How does that phrase about God's "wings" explain everything Ruth has done? (Note the following verses about God's wings: Ex. 19:4; Ps. 36:7; 57:1.)

Boaz prays that God will "repay" Ruth with a "full reward," as she has come to take refuge under *his* wings (Ruth 2:12). Comment on just how that reward is given to Ruth in this chapter.

---

3. Processing the Meeting of Boaz and Ruth (2:17–23)

Naomi forms this chapter's bookends, as Ruth leaves her and then returns to her, carrying about an ephah of barley (over 5 gallons, or 24 liters), along with the leftovers from lunch (vv. 14, 18)! It's a rich and overflowing scene—first with the food and grain, and finally with the amazing news of the source of all this abundance. There is some debate about whose "kindness" (*hesed*) Naomi refers to, in the first statement of verse 20. It certainly could refer to Boaz, but how might it perhaps most fittingly refer to the Lord? And how does this statement represent a reversal of perspective for Naomi, especially in contrast with certain statements in chapter 1?

Next, in verse 20, Naomi informs Ruth that Boaz is one of her family's "redeemers," sometimes called "kinsman-redeemers." Jewish law made provision for a near kinsman to redeem (buy back) land sold by a poverty-stricken relative, and even to redeem the relatives themselves who were sometimes sold into slavery if they had no way to pay their debts. The purpose was to keep the family and the God-given inheritance together (Lev. 25:25–55). At this point in the narrative, the fact that Boaz is a potential redeemer leads to no immediate conclusions. We know nothing so far of Elimelech's land and what has happened to it. And yet, these women have found Boaz, who has shown kindness. Why does the narrator probably hope we'll think back to the wording of Ruth 2:3?

The Lord's kindness never fails. Naomi thought it had. What various factors contributed to her opening her eyes? What can we learn from this, both as we need to see clearly and as we help others see clearly the kind providence of God always at work?

Ruth chapter 3 does not happen the next day! How do the final three verses of chapter 2 make an important transition in the story?

Read through the following three sections on *Gospel Glimpses*, *Whole-Bible Connections*, and *Theological Soundings*. Then take time to consider the *Personal Implications* these sections may have for you.

Gospel Glimpses

REDEMPTION. The redemption which now begins to wind as a strong thread through the rest of the narrative is a concrete historical practice—a legal provision that protected the lives and inheritances of many needy people in Israel. What a mercy that God should have established a way for the poor among his people to be rescued. This story's theme of redemption is a concrete one, but in Scripture's larger context we cannot help but follow this thread toward Jesus our Redeemer. The spiritually charged meaning of redemption grows in the book of Ruth, especially as we watch the narrative point toward the line of David and as we think wonderingly of the Son of David who accomplished for us "redemption through his blood, the forgiveness of our trespasses" (Eph. 1:7).

FAVOR TOWARD THE WEAK. The Bible is full of needy people who receive favor from those who have power to help them. Every such story echoes the big story of needy human beings who receive unmerited favor from God through his Son. Ruth 2 highlights the word *favor* (vv. 2, 10, 13), as this poor foreigner humbly acknowledges her need and her wonder at that need being met with such favor—or such *grace*, as the Hebrew *hen* can also be translated. This word often appears in conjunction with God's *hesed*, his kindness or steadfast love: indeed, Ruth's finding such favor leads Naomi to see that God's "kindness" (*hesed*) "has not forsaken the living or the dead" (2:20).

Whole-Bible Connections

THE MOSAIC LAW. The book of Ruth is rich with reference to laws God established to nurture and protect the poor and needy among his people. Both the laws concerning gleaning in the fields and those concerning redemption of land evidence the Lord's compassion for the needy and his call for his people to extend that same compassion. This story's gospel ramifications help us hold together a concern for both physical human need and the ultimately important spiritual need of every human being for a refuge in the Lord God.

GOD'S WINGS. Not only in the Old Testament do we find pictures of God's wings as our refuge. Jesus looked over Jerusalem and his own people who rejected him, saying, "How often would I have gathered your children together as a hen gathers her brood under her wings, and you were not willing!" (Matt. 23:37). Back in the time of the judges, Ruth points us to the fullness of God's love that, finally rejected by his own people, reaches out to create a people from all the nations of the world.

Theological Soundings

PROVIDENCE. Yes, providence again . . . overflowing! God's providence infuses this story from beginning to end, but in this chapter the pictures of it are especially rich, particularly in relation to harvest plenty. By the time Ruth leaves the field of Boaz which she "happens" upon, she has received more help than the law required (plenteous bread and water and wine, extra grain pulled out and left for her), more lunch than she can eat, and perhaps almost more barley than she can carry home! God's provision is pictured in Scripture not as measured out to be just enough, but rather as overflowing, poured down from the windows of heaven (Mal. 3:10), "good measure, pressed down, shaken together, running over" (Luke 6:38), not just life but "abundant" life (John 10:10). The harvest that God ultimately promises is abundant and eternal (Ps. 126:6; John 4:31–38).

GRACE AND GOOD WORKS. Boaz prays that God will "repay" and "reward" Ruth for her selfless care of her mother-in-law (2:12). A quick reading might lead to the conclusion that Ruth's good works deserve God's good reward—that we somehow earn his favor. The climactic point of verse 12, however, is that what Ruth has done is to take refuge under the wings of the God of Israel. From that place of faith her good deeds have overflowed. Boaz prays she will be blessed not because she has earned any favor but because she has by grace found the place of blessing, in following the true God. Ruth's response of humble servanthood confirms this understanding of her as one who is responding to the grace and favor she receives.

Personal Implications

Take time to reflect on the implications of Ruth 2 for your own life today. Make notes below on the personal implications for your walk with the Lord that you find in the (1) *Gospel Glimpses*, (2) *Whole-Bible Connections*, (3) *Theological Soundings*, and (4) this passage as a whole.

1. Gospel Glimpses

2. Whole-Bible Connections

3. Theological Soundings

4. Ruth 2

As You Finish This Unit . . .

Take a moment now to ask for the Lord's blessing and help as you continue in this study of Ruth. Take a moment also to look back through this unit of study, to reflect on a few key things that the Lord may be teaching you—and perhaps to highlight and underline these things to review again in the future.

Week 4: A Proposal on the Threshing Floor

Ruth 3

▲

The Place of the Passage

Ruth 1 started at a low point, with Naomi alone, bitter, and empty. The return to Bethlehem immediately precipitated a flow of rising action and hope. Ruth 2 added overflowing kindness and more hope, as we were left pondering possible further good from the central encounter of Ruth and Boaz. Naomi clearly has been doing some hopeful pondering! In chapter 3 the hope rises to a climactic moment, which will culminate in the resolution of chapter 4.

The Big Picture

The proposal scene directed by Naomi and gracefully executed by Ruth, on the threshing floor at night, brings joyful resolution—and further hope, related to the desired act of redemption.

> **Reflection and Discussion**

Read slowly through the complete passage, Ruth 3. Then consider and write your reflections on the following questions, which move through the chapter section by section. (For further background, see the *ESV Study Bible*, pages 481–482, or visit esv.org.)

1. Naomi's Plan for Ruth's Rest (3:1–5)

Notice the word "rest" in Ruth 3:1, and recall the context of the same word in Ruth 1:9. How does the use of this word affect our understanding of Ruth 3?

The "threshing floor" was an open-air setting where the harvested sheaves were delivered, the grain was loosened from the straw (often by cattle treading on it), and then the grain was "winnowed," or tossed up with winnowing forks so the wind could blow away the straw and chaff. The men often remained there after a long day of work, eating and drinking—and staying the night to guard the grain. Naomi's plan for Ruth to visit Boaz secretly in the night is presented matter-of-factly and accepted by Ruth with no commentary—but it was an unorthodox plan! What various possible ways of interpreting her plan might you imagine?

2. The Proposal (3:6–14)

The scene, in Ruth 3:6–8, begins dark and full of tension: Ruth is obviously putting herself (and Naomi) at great risk in a number of ways. What have we

28

read so far in this chapter and in this book that might invite us to trust Boaz in this moment of tension?

Ruth must have thought carefully about what to do and say! How does her response to Boaz's startled question in verse 9 actually respond to and interpret his earlier words, in Ruth 2:12? ("Spread your wings" could also be translated "Spread the corners of your garment," but it is important to see Ruth's use of the very word "wings" earlier used by Boaz.)

By so asking for his protection as a "redeemer," Ruth is asking Boaz to redeem *her* along with Elimelech's land—in sort of a "custom" combination of the laws concerning levirate marriage and kinsman redemption. Boaz would have understood that, with this request, Ruth was asking him to marry her. Read and comment on the similar picture in Ezekiel 16:8, where God speaks as the husband of his unfaithful people.

What a magnificent moment, when the "worthy man" (2:1) lives up to our hopes! In Ruth 3:10–14, in what various ways does Boaz honor and protect this "worthy woman" (3:11)? What words stand out?

In what ways are the actions and responses of Boaz and Ruth in this chapter shaped not only by their own characters but also by their knowledge of the other's character?

In fact, the whole town is involved in this scene! Everyone knows, says Boaz, that Ruth is an *eshet khayil* (3:11—Hebrew for "worthy woman," the same words used in Prov. 31:10). How does this chapter (and this book so far) show that love and marriage are intricately connected to the community of God's people?

3. Back Again to Naomi (Ruth 3:15–18)

The ample supply of barley Boaz sends with Ruth is meant to send a message to Naomi! How does this picture of abundance help highlight Naomi's journey through the book?

The chapter opened with Naomi and the search for "rest" for "my daughter" (v. 1). It closes with Naomi and the same themes ("rest," and "my daughter"; v. 18)—but now with the resolution in sight. The pace of the narrative quickens, with the space of only hours between this chapter and the next. Stop and think, at this point, of the worthy man and the worthy woman we have witnessed at the heart of this climactic chapter. What qualities in them stand out, especially in contrast to the "heroes" and "heroines" of many love stories in our world today?

Read through the following three sections on *Gospel Glimpses*, *Whole-Bible Connections*, and *Theological Soundings*. Then take time to consider the *Personal Implications* these sections may have for you.

▶ Gospel Glimpses

REDEMPTION. The theme of redemption grows. This story is full of Ruth's blessedness and wonder at finding such a kind redeemer who is willing not only to pay a price for her but to marry her in love. The pictures this book uses to show such a human redeemer are pictures the Bible uses to show our redeeming God: the one who saves and protects us under his wings (Ruth 2:12; 3:9; Ps. 91:4; Mal. 4:2), the husband who loves and covenants with his wife (Ezek. 16:8; Hos. 2:16–23), and the Son willing to ransom[1] us at his own cost (Matt. 20:28). Boaz's words in Ruth 3:13 ring out: "I will redeem you." As the book progresses and these various pictures merge, the story of Boaz the redeemer resonates increasingly with the Bible's big story of redemption by Christ.

THE FOREIGNER WELCOMED. Ruth portrays the beauty of being redeemed, though not, in this story, by showing any sinfulness of her own from which she is rescued. Of course Ruth was not sinless, and we know that God drew her from a pagan society of idol-worshipers. Ruth is a *foreigner* to Israel, *not part of God's people*, who *becomes part of God's people*. (Read again those beautiful words of Hos. 2:23; also 1 Pet. 2:10). This is what Christ's redemption accomplishes: by grace, through faith, we are reconciled to God and become part of his family forever. Ruth is not called "the Moabite" in this chapter. In this joyful, pastoral harvest setting we sense she has come home and is covered and safe, richly provided for. The public redemption must be resolved, but the private scene is full of satisfying resolution, with Ruth under the wings of Boaz her redeemer.

Whole-Bible Connections

REST. Naomi seeks "rest" for her daughters-in-law (Ruth 1:9; 3:1). This book's picture of rest comes through a woman's eyes, and it comes in the form of a home and a husband and children. The way in which Boaz as a husband/redeemer shows God's husbandry and redemption of his people invites us to consider further biblical connotations of this book's "rest." The theme of the divine gift of *rest* stretches throughout Scripture—repeatedly identified in the Old Testament with the Land of Promise (Josh. 1:13, 15). The writer of Hebrews, however, makes clear that Joshua was not able to give the people rest by bringing them into the land; only through the work of Jesus on our behalf can we find the "Sabbath rest" that belongs to the people of God (Heb. 4:1–10). The rest given to Ruth by Boaz not only points to the ultimate rest provided by Christ our Redeemer; it also continues the line that leads to his birth and to true, eternal rest for God's people.

WORTHY WOMEN. The words with which Boaz praises Ruth bring to mind the words of Proverbs 31. (The matching *eshet khayil* has been noted in Ruth 3:11 and Prov. 31:10.) Certainly Ruth shows the same faith, industry, and family devotion the wisdom literature celebrates. In the Hebrew Bible the book of Ruth followed Proverbs, so the connections might have been more noticeable. Proverbs 31:31 concludes, "Let her works praise her in the gates." The same Hebrew word for "gate" is found in Ruth 3:11, where "all my fellow townsmen" translates two words meaning literally "gate" and "people." The gathering place of a town's people, of course, was at the town's gate—where both literally and figuratively the good works of a worthy woman would be known and praised. (This will happen literally for Ruth in the next chapter!) It is helpful to see Ruth in a larger biblical progression of "holy women who hoped in God," doing good and not fearing anything that is frightening (1 Pet. 3:1–6).

Theological Soundings

WORTHINESS AND UNWORTHINESS. It is tempting to focus so much on the worthiness of this virtuous man and woman that we forget the kind providence of God directing and enabling every moment of their story. The Proverbs 31 "worthy woman" is worthy only because she embodies the wisdom given by God to his people in his kingdom: God's "kindness" (*hesed*; Prov. 31:26) is on her tongue and in her heart. So with Ruth and Boaz: they are in the place God has mercifully visited (Ruth 1:6), supplying their needs and making them part of his people. Ruth and Boaz are two *humbly* virtuous characters, both of whom receive more than what they know they deserve—Ruth as a foreigner (2:10) and Boaz as an older man whom young Ruth chooses to love rather than going after young men (3:10). Both Boaz and Ruth have taken refuge under God's kind wings, and they know it. From that place, they acknowledge and pass on the kindness of the Lord himself. That is their worthiness.

MARRIAGE AND SEXUAL PURITY IN RELATION TO GOD. God made male and female from the beginning to enjoy sexual purity in relation to marriage, the faithful marriage of a husband and a wife (Gen. 1–2). Clearly, this purity is at the heart of who we are meant to be—so much so, that such purity is used to picture the faithful obedience to which God calls his people. Biblical imagery for the rebellion of God's people is often that of whoredom, or sexual infidelity (Isa. 1:21; Hos. 9:1). We must say that God washes all sin clean, through the blood of Christ, as we return to him. He purifies his people; he makes his bride beautiful (Rev. 19:7–8; 21:2). But we must say, too, that Scripture offers a strong call to sexual purity. God's people are to offer the most beautiful pictures of him in the way we live as sexual beings (either in the sexual relations within marriage, or in sexual celibacy outside of marriage). The book of Ruth vividly shows such purity, as a man with a merry heart and a woman freshly washed and scented meet alone under the night sky and restrain themselves in preparation for marriage. Ruth and Boaz had not read but evidently knew the weight of Paul's teaching in 1 Thessalonians 4:1–8.

Personal Implications

Take time to reflect on the implications of Ruth 3 for your own life today. Make notes below on the personal implications you find for your walk with the Lord in the (1) *Gospel Glimpses*, (2) *Whole-Bible Connections*, (3) *Theological Soundings*, and (4) this passage as a whole.

1. Gospel Glimpses

2. Whole-Bible Connections

3. Theological Soundings

4. Ruth 3

As You Finish This Unit . . .

Take a moment now to ask for the Lord's blessing and help as you continue in this study of Ruth. Take a moment also to look back through this unit of study, to reflect on a few key things that the Lord may be teaching you—and perhaps to highlight and underline these things to review again in the future.

Definition

[1] **Ransom** – A price paid to redeem, or buy back, someone who had become enslaved or something that had been lost to someone else. Jesus described his ministry as serving others and giving his life as a ransom for many (Mark 10:45).

Week 5: Redemption at the Gate

Ruth 4

▲

The Place of the Passage

The book's final chapter not only joyfully resolves the question of whether Boaz will have first right to redeem Ruth and give her rest. It also resolves the whole story's movement: from Naomi's initial bitter emptiness, to her final lapful of blessing and joy. The concluding section reaches out to an even greater resolution of redemption accomplished by the Son of David.

The Big Picture

Layers of blessing unfold as the story resolves: the nearer kinsman bows out and leaves Ruth to Boaz, their marriage produces a son, the reversal of Naomi's emptiness is complete, and we glimpse the line of this child reaching all the way to King David.

> ## Reflection and Discussion

Read carefully through Ruth 4. Then consider and write your reflections on the following questions, which move through the chapter and conclude the book. (For further background, see the *ESV Study Bible*, pages 482–483, or visit esv.org.)

1. Who Will Be the Redeemer? (4:1–6)

The previous chapter called for a quick resolution! How do the details of the narrative (and of Boaz's method) impress you, in verses 1–6? Why is this process so important?

The closer kinsman-redeemer with first rights (whose name is not recorded or remembered) quickly changes his yes to no! Why? What does he fear? What is the irony here, in light of the rest of the chapter?

2. The Redeemer Accomplishes the Redemption (4:7–12)

With the exchanged sandal symbolizing the transferred rights to redemption, Boaz legitimately and nobly announces his redemption of Elimelech's inheritance. How do his words show that he understands the purpose of the laws he is fulfilling?

Trace the repeated mentions of the various people gathered in this scene, which is "bookended" not by Naomi this time, but by the larger gathering of the elders. In what ways is it important that this is not just a private but a public resolution?

The elders' blessing concluding this scene asks God to prosper Boaz and Ruth as he has done for his people in the past. First, briefly review a bit of the history to which they refer: of Rachel and Leah (Gen. 29–30); of Perez, Tamar, and Judah (Gen. 38; Matt. 1:1–6). What elements of this history stand out in relation to this story?

As you read this blessing given at the city's gate (vv. 11–12), how do the words and phrases echo even more loudly than the people could know at the time?

3. The Bookends of the Book: Back to Naomi (4:13–17)

How is the view of God expressed in Ruth 4:13–17 both similar to and different from the view expressed by Naomi in chapter 1? In what ways does this concluding scene perfectly complete the shape of Naomi's story?

Verses 14–15 speak about the newborn son as a "redeemer." In what ways does this title fit this particular child?

4. Conclusion and Conclusions (4:18–22)

Ruth 4:13–17 actually makes a good conclusion for the narrative. Why then go on to add an official (and slightly repetitive) genealogy? This genealogy in Ruth 4:18–22 looks both back and forward, from Boaz's time. First, read Genesis 49:8–10; Isaiah 11:1–2, 10; Matthew 1:1–17; and Revelation 5:1–5. Then write your thoughts musing on the wonder of a book about Ruth set in the time of the judges and ending (twice!) with the name of David (vv. 17, 21).

We have described Ruth as *the story of a God who provides for his people according to his promises.* Look back one more time to the promises given to Abraham in Genesis 12:1–7. In light of these verses, write your summary of how the book of Ruth shows a God who provides for his people according to his promises.

Read through the following three sections on *Gospel Glimpses, Whole-Bible Connections,* and *Theological Soundings.* Then take time to consider the *Personal Implications* these sections may have for you.

Gospel Glimpses

REDEMPTION PURCHASED. We have seen the theme of redemption develop throughout Ruth, but in the final scene we watch it enacted, as Boaz *buys* from Naomi all that belonged to her sons—including Ruth. This cost of redemption, paid in full, points to another, greater Redeemer, Jesus Christ, who ransomed us "from the futile ways inherited from your forefathers, not with perishable things such as silver or gold, but with the precious blood of Christ, like that of a lamb without blemish or spot" (1 Pet. 1:18–19).

JOYFUL PRAISE OF GOD'S PEOPLE. The closing scenes offer marvelous pictures of God's people together rejoicing in his steadfast love and saving kindness. The women's "Blessed be the Lord" (Ruth 4:14) joins a chorus of generations of praise and worship to a redeeming God. Truly, as Mary sang, "his mercy is for those who fear him from generation to generation" (Luke 1:50). In the words of Zechariah, "Blessed be the Lord God of Israel, for he has visited and redeemed his people and has raised up a horn of salvation for us in the house of his servant David" (Luke 1:68–69).

GRACE. One cannot help but notice, even in a cursory review of Israel's history referenced in Ruth 4:11–12, that the story of God's people is full of sin and brokenness. How remarkable to celebrate Ruth's joyful marriage and childbearing in light of the marriage/childbirth stories of Rachel, Leah, and Tamar! And yet God's grace wove eternal blessing out of all these imperfect relationships, according to his kind, unfailing promises. Each of these families needed, benefited from, and helped lead the way toward the perfect grace to be found in Jesus our Redeemer.

Whole-Bible Connections

GOD GIVING CONCEPTION. Ruth 4:13 makes it clear that God gave conception to Ruth, who had been barren for 10 years. The Bible shows a long line of barren women whose wombs God opened, in his perfect timing: Sarah (Gen. 21:1–2); Rachel and Leah (Gen. 29:31–30:24); Hannah (1 Sam. 1); Elizabeth (Luke 1:5–25). In these stories we see a God who "gives the barren woman a home, making her the joyous mother of children" (Ps. 113:9). Such mercy, however, is meant to point us to a God who is working his redemptive purposes—

amazingly, even through his sovereign management of women's wombs. In the presence of the very first woman was heard the promise that her seed would destroy the evil one (Gen. 3:15). In the whole process of human conception, God's redemptive purposes are at work, generation after generation.

GENEALOGIES. Ruth 4:18–22 is one link in a whole biblical network of genealogies, beginning early in Genesis (4:17–22). Biblical history traces Noah's descendants to Abraham, Abraham's descendants through his 12 sons and eventually through the tribe of Judah to David, and finally David's line to the promised Christ. God's people understood that his promises were to be delivered through promised offspring—and so they traced and traced that offspring. Matthew's opening genealogy (1:1–17) summarizes the tracing, culminating in Jesus Christ.

A PEOPLE FROM EVERY TRIBE AND NATION. As Ruth the Moabite is enfolded among God's people and into the messianic line,[1] this story leaves us celebrating God's promise to bless "all the families of the earth" through Abraham's seed (Gen. 12:3). That promise bursts into fulfillment in the New Testament, especially as in Acts we see the gospel going out "to the end of the earth" (Acts 1:8). But the fulfillment was happening all along, as we see in stories like those of Rahab (Joshua 2) and Ruth. Jonah didn't like the idea. Isaiah makes it clear (Isa. 2:2–3). The Gospels make it abundantly clear (John 1:12–13). The book of Revelation shows the glorious end result (Rev. 5:9–10).

▶ Theological Soundings

OBEDIENCE TO GOD'S LAW. Boaz in the redemption scene is careful to observe and articulate in painstaking detail the Mosaic laws concerning redemption of land and relatives. In his redeemer role Boaz shows the fulfillment of God's law—just as Christ our Redeemer perfectly fulfilled God's law during his earthly life, in order to be able perfectly to secure our redemption. Boaz consistently does even more than the law requires: he gives Ruth not only the proper gleanings but all sorts of extra attention and provision as well, and of course he finally pursues marriage to her, though he is not technically required to do so. So, in Christ our Redeemer, God's perfect law and his unending love meet.

INHERITANCE. The book of Ruth, especially in this final chapter, highlights the importance of preserving one's family inheritance (Ruth 4:5, 6, 10). The inheritance of every Israelite was one given by God, originally administered through Joshua to the 12 tribes as they settled in the Promised Land. That rich inheritance offers a picture of every believer's ultimate inheritance through Christ's redemption of us (1 Pet. 1:3–5): this is the "beautiful inheritance" David glimpsed and celebrated in Psalm 16:5–6.

Personal Implications

Take time to reflect on the implications of Ruth 4 for your own life today. Make notes below on the personal implications for your walk with the Lord that you find in the (1) *Gospel Glimpses*, (2) *Whole-Bible Connections*, (3) *Theological Soundings*, and (4) this passage as a whole.

1. Gospel Glimpses

2. Whole-Bible Connections

3. Theological Soundings

4. Ruth 4

As You Finish This Unit . . .

Take a moment now to ask for the Lord's blessing and help as you continue in this study, moving from Ruth to Esther. Take a moment also to look back through this unit of study, to reflect on a few key things that the Lord may be teaching you—and perhaps to highlight and underline these things to review again in the future.

Definition

[1] **Messiah** – Transliteration of a Hebrew word meaning "anointed one," the equivalent of the Greek word *Christ*. Originally applied to anyone specially designated for a particular role, such as king or priest. Jesus himself affirmed that he was the Messiah sent from God (Matt. 16:16–17).

WEEK 6: OVERVIEW OF ESTHER

Getting Acquainted

We move now from one biblical book named after a woman to the other one. Ruth lived a few generations before King David, as we have seen; Esther lived after the great kingdom of Israel had risen and fallen. Ruth was a foreigner who found her home in a small Judean town surrounded by fields of grain; Esther was a Jew who found herself living in the royal courts of the Persian empire, surrounded by luxury. The books reflect their settings: Ruth's story has the simplicity of a pastoral tale, but Esther's is an ornate and complexly shaped narrative. Different as they are, the stories of both women point to a Lord God who steadfastly fulfills his promises to his people.

The narrative method of Esther points to this God in a unique way—without ever mentioning him! Ruth's characters show by their actions and dialogue that they know and serve the God of Israel; Esther's characters are woven into a plot that shows by its very shape the amazing redemptive pattern in human events. There are no grand miracles[1] in Esther and no rehearsing of God's blessings. Set far from the land where God promised to dwell with his people, there is no temple,[2] no public worship, no obvious sense of God at work. The question is: *is* he at work, when we can't see him or even hear his name? The book of Esther shows that he is. *Esther is a story of God's remarkable providence in shaping human events, according to his promises, for the blessing of his people and the destruction of their enemies.* (For further background, see the *ESV Study Bible*, pages 849–852, or visit esv.org.)

Placing It in the Larger Story

Just like Ruth, Esther lights up the context of God's promises to Abraham in Genesis 12:1–3—not only that from him would come a great nation, but also that God would bless those who bless him and curse those who dishonor him (and, by implication, the nation to come from him). By Esther's time we have also the historical context of God's covenant with David (2 Sam. 7:12–17), which included the promise of an eternal kingdom in his line. All these promises seem threatened in the book of Esther. God's people had rebelled against him under their earthly kings, their kingdom had split and fallen, and its people had been taken into exile.[3] Even though in Esther's time that exile had officially ended, only a remnant[4] of Jews had returned, as subjects of the Persian empire, to a broken-down Jerusalem. This story brings what seems the final blow: on a certain day, by the Persian king's edict, all Jews throughout the empire (which included Jerusalem) are to be annihilated. Where is God? Where is the king he promised? What about God's promises?

The book of Esther tells of the overturning of this cruel threat through Esther's courage and ultimately through a myriad of providential occurrences unfolded by the plot. In a masterfully patterned narrative that pivots right in the center, we see God's people in the depths but then exalted, and their enemies high and proud but then brought down. This is the very gospel pattern of reversal sung about by women like Hannah (1 Sam. 2:1–10) and Mary (Luke 1:46–55). God's promises are true, and they are true ultimately in the promised King who came down to earth, down to the lowest point of death on a cross, and then rose from the dead and ascended to the heights of heaven—the great reversal, which makes possible our own reversal from death to eternal life.

Key Verse

"Now in the twelfth month, which is the month of Adar, on the thirteenth day of the same, when the king's command and edict were about to be carried out, on the very day when the enemies of the Jews hoped to gain the mastery over them, the reverse occurred: the Jews gained mastery over those who hated them" (Est. 9:1).

Date and Historical Background

Esther's story takes place in Susa, capital of the Persian empire, during the reign of King Ahasuerus (or Xerxes, in Greek), who ruled from 485 to 464 BC. When Judah fell to the Babylonian King Nebuchadnezzar in 586 BC, Jerusalem was destroyed and God's people were taken as exiles to Babylon. But in 539 BC., Persian King Cyrus conquered Babylon and released the exiles to return to their land. Some Jews did not return—including Esther's family. We find Esther and her cousin, Mordecai, settled in the Persian empire and in fact right under the nose of this later and very powerful Persian king.

The author and date of composition of Esther are unknown, although the original text indicates an author close to the time of the events, one with an intimate knowledge of the story's setting and details.

Outline

I. Introduction: The Pieces in Place (1:1–2:23)

   A. Queen Vashti's downfall (1:1–22)

   B. Esther's rise to the throne (2:1–18)

   C. Mordecai's success in foiling a plot against the king (2:19–23)

II. Main Action: A Great Reversal (3:1– 9:19)

   A. God's people falling; enemies rising (3:1–5:14)

      1. The crisis: Haman plots to kill the Jews (3:1–15)
      2. Mordecai and Esther plan to save their people (4:1–17)
      3. Esther is favorably received by the king; Esther's first feast (5:1–8)
      4. Haman prepares to hang Mordecai (5:9–14)

   B. God's people rising; enemies falling (6:1–9:19)

      1. A pivotal night; Mordecai is honored and Haman is humiliated (6:1–13)
      2. Esther's second feast; Haman's destruction (6:14–7:10)
      3. Esther wins the right of the Jews to defend themselves (8:1–17)
      4. The Jews completely destroy their enemies (9:1–19)

III. Conclusion (9:20–10:3)

   A. The establishment of the Feast of Purim (9:20–32)

   B. Mordecai's high rank and beneficent rule (10:1–3)

> ## As You Get Started . . .

Do a quick read-through of Esther, as if you were reading a short story. What aspects of the book stand out after such a reading?

Esther is a highly patterned narrative. Many have noticed, for example, the theme of feasting, or banqueting, that winds through the book. Do your own search for the progression of feasts or banquets from beginning to end. What do you observe?

What several themes of the book might you identify at this early point? Does any one of them stand out as central? Why or why not?

Esther is an intriguing heroine. What general observations would you make or questions would you ask about her, at this point? As we begin this study, what questions do you have about this book?

As You Finish This Unit . . .

Take a moment now to ask God to bless you with increased understanding and a transformed heart and life as you study the book of Esther. Look back through this introductory chapter and underline words or thoughts you would like to pray about or consider further. May the Spirit who inspired Scripture's living and active words use them to challenge and encourage your heart.

Definitions

[1] **Miracle** – A special act of God that goes beyond natural means, thus demonstrating God's power.

[2] **Temple** – A place set aside as holy because of God's presence there. Solomon built the first temple of the Lord in Jerusalem, to replace the portable tabernacle. This temple was later destroyed by the Babylonians, rebuilt, and destroyed again by the Romans.

[3] **Exile** – The forced relocation of large groups of people, usually in times of war. In biblical studies, "the exile" typically refers to the Babylonian exile, that is, Nebuchadnezzar's relocation of residents of the southern kingdom of Judah to Babylon in 586 BC. (Residents of the northern kingdom of Israel had been resettled by Assyria in 722 BC.) After Babylon came under Persian rule, several waves of Jewish exiles returned and repopulated Judah.

[4] **Remnant** – A remnant chosen by God and saved by grace is a theme that runs throughout the Bible. When God judged the earth with a flood, he saved Noah's family through the ark (Gen. 6:17–18). In the time of Elijah God kept seven thousand from committing idolatry (1 Kings 19:18). When the prophets looked forward to God's salvation after exile, their hope was that a faithful remnant would be saved (Mic. 4:6–7; Zeph. 3:12). When Christ came, he began to gather this remnant to himself. When he returns, he will gather his scattered, now multiethnic people, to himself.

WEEK 7: THE PIECES IN PLACE

Esther 1–2

▲

The Place of the Passage

The opening chapters of Esther are a bit like the elegant opening moves of a chess game, in which the direction and movement are established, with each piece in its position. As we enter this decadent Persian court, King Ahasuerus is introduced in all his royal but ineffective pomp; Queen Vashti is deposed and Queen Esther crowned; and Esther's cousin Mordecai serves the king and foils a plot against him. All these "pieces" of the plot must be in place just so, in order for the action to proceed as it does throughout the rest of the book. What seems like a self-contained drama in the palace of King Ahasuerus is really the introduction to a much larger drama, one that stretches as far as the survival of God's people.

The Big Picture

Chapters 1–2 immerse us in the extravagance of King Ahasuerus's court, where, against the background of lavish feasts and decadent beauty rituals, Queen Vashti falls and Queen Esther rises.

> ### Reflection and Discussion

Read through the complete passage for this study, Esther 1–2. Then consider and write your reflections on the following questions, which move through this introductory section of Esther. (For further background, see the *ESV Study Bible*, pages 853–856, or visit esv.org.)

1. The King, His Feasts, and His Queen (Esther 1)

The book opens with a pair of sumptuous feasts given by the king (1:3, 5). Many think this passage portrays the time in which Persian King Xerxes was preparing for his famous invasion of Greece in 480 BC (in which he was soundly defeated). After reading Esther 1:1–9, how would you finish this sentence: "The book of Esther starts out by . . . ? What details stand out to you in this opening section?

Now read the rest of chapter 1. In contrast to the first section (and a little closer up), how does the king come across in verses 10–22? Offer specific verses that support your answer.

Especially in light of Scripture's teaching about the beauties of submission and headship in marriage (as in Eph. 5:22–33), in what various ways is this story of the king's decree ironically distorted, even ridiculous? What are we learning here about this king and his decrees?

Clearly, this king and this kingdom treated women abominably. We would all like to know Vashti's thoughts and feelings on that subject—but we don't get to; that is clearly not the narrator's purpose. Think of several reasons why this background story of Queen Vashti is important to the flow of the whole book. Why is it crucial and enlightening to have this episode first?

2. Enter Esther and Mordecai (Esther 2)

We do not know what Esther was thinking and feeling. According to your careful observations of chapter 2, make two lists: first, what can be known for sure about the heroine of this book; and, second, what you would like to know but can't.

What general observations can you make about the narrative method of telling this story?

The luxurious beauty treatments sound nice . . . but consider their implications in this story. What details in chapter 2 reveal the true nature of the world in which Esther finds herself? Give your own nutshell description of this harem.

Many have noted that Esther throughout this chapter is being "done unto" rather than doing, obeying rather than initiating. What details in the text confirm this observation?

One thing Esther does: *win favor*. Consider these words:

- in verse 9: "favor" (Hebrew *hesed*);
- in verse 15: "favor" (Hebrew *hen*);
- in verse 17: "grace and favor" (Hebrew *hesed* and *hen*).

Now, think back: in Ruth 1–2, the words "favor" (Hebrew *hen*) and "kindness" (Hebrew *hesed*) pointed us to God's steadfast love for his covenant people (see Week 2 *Whole Bible Connections*; and Week 3, *Gospel Glimpses*). Find these same words in Joseph's story, Genesis 39:21–23. The "favor" found by Daniel is the same *hesed* (Dan. 1:8–9). Here's the question: what similarities do you see in the circumstances of Esther, Ruth, Joseph, and Daniel?

Of course, we are not told that the favor Esther won came from God. We are reminded repeatedly, however, of the people to whom Esther belongs. Find those reminders in the chapter; what is their effect?

_____

_____

_____

_____

_____

Esther 2:19–23 focuses finally on Mordecai, whose "sitting at the king's gate" indicates a position of official service to the king. The plot he foils shows how strategic his position is. In all these events, God has not been mentioned, but his hand of providence is clearly at work. Step back and review all the things that have had to happen just so, so far.

_____

_____

_____

_____

_____

Read through the following three sections on *Gospel Glimpses, Whole-Bible Connections,* and *Theological Soundings.* Then take time to consider the *Personal Implications* these sections may have for you.

Gospel Glimpses

HUMAN DEPRAVITY.[1] In one sense, the gospel looms large in this book through its display of the lostness of lives without it. Esther opens in a world seemingly without God—certainly without any mention of God—and ruled by those who do not know him. It is a world where people are not just foolish in their thinking but also cruel in their treatment of others, especially the weak and vulnerable (a conquered minority evidently afraid to identify themselves, a subjugated sex with no means of protecting themselves). Amid the glitz of the Persian empire we see those described by the apostle Paul: "... they became futile in their thinking, and their foolish hearts were darkened" (Rom. 1:21). This is a world that needs a much greater king than the great Ahasuerus.

FAVOR. As we have noted, the "grace and favor" flowing in Esther's direction connect with a larger scriptural pattern of God's steadfast love promised and consistently shown to his people. This covenant kindness was promised to the people through whom would come the promised Seed, the Messiah—and God's promises do not fail. His people, the Jews, still existed as Jews even after decades of dispersion in exile. God sent his favor often through the goodwill of those in authority over them. Notwithstanding the alien, godless context of Esther's story, we cannot fail to notice these indications of God's unfailing and steadfast love for his people.

Whole-Bible Connections

EXILE. Without mentioning the Jews' God, the writer makes clear the historical context of the Jews' exile from their land. Esther 2:5–6 three times mentions the Jews' being "carried away" from Jerusalem by Babylonian King Nebuchadnezzar. Esther is crafted as a complete but not an independent narrative; its story is firmly embedded in the whole story of God's chosen people who grew from Abraham into a great kingdom, and who lost that kingdom as they disobeyed God, were conquered, and suffered in exile. By Esther's time, the exile is officially over, just as God had promised (Jer. 25:11–14; 32:36–38). The explicit context of the exile connects the Jews to their God, and to God's promises as far back as Abraham (Gen. 12:1–3)—and as far ahead as Abraham's promised Seed, the ultimate Deliverer and the heavenly King.

HEADSHIP AND SUBMISSION IN MARRIAGE. False, flattering assertions concerning the king's sovereignty lead to ridiculous conclusions, such as that Queen Vashti's behavior will inspire all the kingdom's wives to rebel—or that King Ahasuerus's decree will compel them all to honor the "master" of the household (1:17–22). The distance between the story's reality and the biblical ideal is so far as to be almost laughable. Many other Scriptures will help us, but Esther will not, if we want to do a study on godly marriage. The themes are clearly there, but this story focuses on the plot unfolding, in which God's people are under the rule of an ungodly king yet still under the hand of a sovereign God. Perhaps the weakness of the Persian sovereign serves best to point to the need for a far better one.

Theological Soundings

SOVEREIGNTY. Kings in the Bible story are supposed to rule their kingdoms with a sovereign hand. In the book of Esther, King Ahasuerus rules the great Persian empire with a show of sovereign power that is satirically exposed, again and again, to be only a show. The king who apparently controls even the drinking habits of his party guests cannot control his own wife's behavior. And to decide how to handle her, he needs seven wise men—who tell him what to do and he does it! This king's sovereignty is potent in its harmful ramifications for the lives of his subjects but pathetic in its foolish ineptitude. Our thoughts might turn by contrast toward the "blessed and only Sovereign, the King of kings and Lord of lords" (1 Tim. 6:15), who perfectly weaves together the events of this story—and of human history.

KINGDOM. The book of Esther takes us into the heart of a kingdom. Even though King Ahasuerus doesn't know it, his is just one of many kingdoms the Bible describes as rising and falling by the hand of the Lord for his redemptive purposes. The prophet Isaiah foretold God's sovereign plan for the rise to power of Xerxes's predecessor Cyrus (Isa. 44:24–45:7). Esther 2:5–6 alludes to three dead kings: first, by implication, King Saul, the most famous "son of Kish, a Benjaminite" (see 1 Sam. 9); second, King Jeconiah, the Judean king who was carried away from his own disintegrating kingdom; and King Nebuchadnezzar, who ruled the great Babylonian empire (before it was conquered by Cyrus). In contrast to all these fleeting earthly kingdoms is the one ruled by the God of heaven, who directs the course of nations from his heavenly throne—and who sent his own Son, King Jesus, to bring in his kingdom and to redeem his people[2] (Mark 1:14–15). The biblical context of kingdoms puts this Persian one in its proper place.

► Personal Implications

Take time to reflect on the implications of Esther 1–2 for your own life today. Make notes below on the personal implications for your walk with the Lord that you find in the (1) *Gospel Glimpses*, (2) *Whole-Bible Connections*, (3) *Theological Soundings*, and (4) this passage as a whole.

1. Gospel Glimpses

----

2. Whole-Bible Connections

----

3. Theological Soundings

4. Esther 1–2

As You Finish This Unit . . .

Take a moment now to ask for the Lord's blessing and help as you continue in this study of Esther. Take a moment also to look back through this unit of study, to reflect on a few key things that the Lord may be teaching you—and perhaps to highlight and underline these things to review again in the future.

Definitions

[1] **Depravity** – The sinful condition of human nature apart from grace, whereby humans are inclined to serve their own will and desires and to reject God's rule.

[2] **Kingdom of God/heaven** – The sovereign rule of God. At the present time, the fallen, sinful world does not belong to the kingdom of God, since it does not submit to God's rule. Instead, God's kingdom can be found in heaven and among his people (Matt. 6:9–10; Luke 17:20–21). After Christ returns, however, the kingdoms of the world will become the kingdom of God (Rev. 11:15). Then all people will, either willingly or regretfully, acknowledge his sovereignty (Phil. 2:9–11). Even the natural world will be transformed to operate in perfect harmony with God (Rom. 8:19–23).

WEEK 8: THE CRISIS AND THE RESPONSE

Esther 3–4

The Place of the Passage

After the introductory chapters set the pieces in place, chapter 3 introduces the crisis that the rest of the book must resolve. Haman enters as the "villain" of the narrative, who sets in motion a plan to annihilate the Jews throughout the empire. Chapter 4, however, sets something else in motion: the character of Esther, whose resolve in this chapter directs the action to its final resolution—at least from a human perspective. These two chapters establish the fundamental tension of the book: the battle between God's people and the enemies of God's people. Even this early on, we sense the larger context of the history and reality of God's promises to his people.

The Big Picture

Chapters 3–4 introduce the crisis (Haman's plot to annihilate the Jews) and Esther's decision to respond, which initiates the process of resolution.

> ## Reflection and Discussion

Read the entire text for this week's study, Esther 3–4. Then consider and write your reflections on the following questions, which move through this section of Esther. (For further background, see the *ESV Study Bible*, pages 856–858, or visit esv.org.)

1. The Villain and the Crisis (Esther 3)

After the final section of chapter 2, whom would you expect to be promoted by King Ahasuerus? Write a character sketch of the one who *was* promoted, according to careful observation of chapter 3.

Historical background is relevant to the tension between Mordecai the Jew and "Haman the Agagite" (3:1). After Mordecai's introduction as a descendant of King Saul (2:5), Haman's introduction likewise links him to a king—an enemy of King Saul. First, read the background story in 1 Samuel 15. Then read the further background in Exodus 17:8–16. We don't know how directly this history influenced the characters in Esther, but in any case the background is clearly there for readers of Scripture. How does this historical context give perspective to the conflict between Mordecai and Haman?

The casting of the lots takes place five years after Esther became queen. Lots were cast in the first month of the year, and the lot fell on the twelfth month as the month in which the Jews were to be destroyed. Along with the Persian word *pur*, the writer gives the Hebrew word "lots" (3:7)—which resonates with other

Old Testament uses of this word. Read Joshua 18:1–10 and Proverbs 16:33. What different perspectives might you discern concerning the casting of lots?

According to Esther 3:12, the king's edict went out on the thirteenth day of the first month, which would have been Passover eve for the Jews (see Ex. 12:18). Compare and contrast the situation described in chapter 3 with the events surrounding the first Passover (review Ex. 12:1–28).

2. Esther's Resolve (Esther 4)

What details of the narrative in Esther 4:1–9 show both the dramatic response of the Jews—and Esther's distance from the Jews, at this point?

Verse 10 of chapter 4 is a turning point in the narrative's presentation of Esther. What things do we for the very first time see Esther doing, in the second half of this chapter?

59

Esther's first response is one of understandable shock and incredulity, as she processes the personal ramifications (v. 11). Consider Mordecai's response to her, in verses 13–14. First, what various arguments does he lay out against her keeping silent? On what assumptions do these arguments seem to rest?

Mordecai's famous final statement in verse 14 offers the *positive* argument. What assumptions are at work in this "Who knows . . ."? To what is Mordecai turning Esther's thoughts here?

Mordecai's appeal reaches the target: Esther's next response is strong and resolved. What various assumptions might we glimpse in her words, in verses 15–16? (Note that, for the Jews, the activity of fasting was almost always associated with and accompanied by prayer.)

The rest of the story grows from this moment of resolve on the part of Esther. Step back for a moment and consider how the circumstances of this moment depend on God's hand of providence at work. Summarize the ways in which we see God's divine direction at this point in the story.

Read through the following three sections on *Gospel Glimpses*, *Whole-Bible Connections*, and *Theological Soundings*. Then take time to consider the *Personal Implications* these sections may have for you.

Gospel Glimpses

CONDEMNED TO DEATH. Esther is all about a people condemned to death by an irrevocable edict of the king. The desperation of their need is emphasized by the edict's instruction "to destroy, to kill, and to annihilate" all the Jews. Without a deliverer this people is hopeless and helpless. The story might lead us to ponder the desperate need of all fallen human beings apart from the deliverance sent to us in Christ who suffered our sentence of death, in our place, on the cross.

A NEEDED INTERCESSOR.[1] Repeatedly throughout Scripture, God's people need someone to represent them, or plead their cause. They are helpless, and by themselves will perish. Moses perhaps most directly offers a type of such an intercessor, a godly leader pleading with the Lord on behalf of a people facing the judgment of death (Ex. 32:7–14). Esther's story suggests a similar pattern, as she is called to "go to the king to beg his favor and plead with him on behalf of her people" (4:8). To be sure, no imperfect human intercessor can come close to picturing the needed perfect One who can fully and finally save. This pattern of needed intercession for a people points us ultimately to the Lord Jesus, whose blood shed on the cross pleads for us, and who even now lives to make intercession for us at the right hand of God the Father in heaven (Rom. 8:34; Heb. 7:25).

Whole-Bible Connections

OPPRESSION OF GOD'S PEOPLE. God's people know and have known oppression from the world around, not just against individuals but against God's people as a whole. His promises were to Abraham's seed, and the threats come repeatedly against that seed—that is, the race Abraham fathered. Haman "disdained to lay hands on Mordecai alone," but "sought to destroy all the Jews, the people of Mordecai, throughout the whole kingdom of Ahasuerus" (3:6). This response to Mordecai's refusal to bow seems dramatically out of proportion; it represents not only personal vengefulness but also a larger, ongoing battle against the people of God. God's declared "war with Amalek from generation to generation" (Ex. 17:16) implies generations of attacks on his people. The pattern continues: Jesus told his followers they would be hated and persecuted even as he was (John 15:18–25)—until that day when he comes again to judge the world and to dwell forever with his people.

FASTING AND PRAYER. The mention of fasting in Esther 4:3, 16 almost certainly implies the accompanying activity of prayer. Among many prophets who call for fasting and heartfelt prayer, Joel offers a pertinent example, as he in the midst of national calamity extended God's call for his people to return to him "with fasting, with weeping, and with mourning" (Joel 2:12). The New Testament as well carries the theme of fasting and prayer: for example, the prophetess Anna worshiped "with fasting and prayer night and day" (Luke 2:37); the believers in Acts 13:2 "were worshiping the Lord and fasting." The broader biblical context of fasting helps us see the never-mentioned but sovereignly active God at work in this book, faithfully watching over his people—and hearing their prayers.

Theological Soundings

PROVIDENCE. God's hand of providence is all over this story. How ironic that it should be a seemingly random casting of lots that so specifically evidences God's superintending hand: the fact that the lot falls 11 months away allows time for deliverance to be worked out according to God's plan. Haman depended on lots in his plot against God's people, while that people's God actually determined how the lots would fall (compare Prov. 16:33). God has clearly determined the position of Mordecai in the service of the king, close to Esther—who is indeed placed in the palace, as Mordecai says, "for such a time as this." This is the story of a great and evil threat, but the unfolding of the story's events shows an overriding good hand of providence.

WORSHIP AND IDOLATRY. Almost like a refrain, three times is mentioned the order to "bow down and pay homage" to Haman (3:2, 5). He wanted to be worshiped. He wanted to be like God. This book shows multiple efforts of human beings to raise themselves to a godlike position. King Ahasuerus tried to do so, as the ruler of a great empire—although we have seen his inability to rule. In chapter 3, he seems like a pawn in the hand of Haman, acquiescing without question to Haman's desires. Haman himself is not so impotent, but he is evil, grasping power in order to satisfy his own prideful, vengeful desires. The Bible tells us we were created to worship the one true God, the only one worthy of our worship. All the puffed-up, would-be gods demanding worship in this book make us long to see him.

Personal Implications

Take time to reflect on the implications of Esther 3–4 for your own life today. Make notes below on the personal implications for your walk with the Lord that you find in the (1) *Gospel Glimpses*, (2) *Whole-Bible Connections*, (3) *Theological Soundings*, and (4) this passage as a whole.

1. Gospel Glimpses

2. Whole-Bible Connections

3. Theological Soundings

4. Esther 3–4

As You Finish This Unit . . .

Take a moment now to ask for the Lord's blessing and help as you continue in this study of Esther. Take a moment also to look back through this unit of study, to reflect on a few key things that the Lord may be teaching you—and perhaps to highlight and underline these things to review again in the future.

Definitions

[1] **Intercessor** – One who appeals to one person on behalf of another. We often speak of intercession with reference to prayer. For believers, Jesus is our great intercessor in heaven with the Father on our behalf.

Week 9: The Story Takes a Turn

Esther 5–6

The Place of the Passage

At the center of the book we find its turning point, when Haman, the enemy of God's people, reaches his high point but then begins to fall, and Mordecai, the sentenced-to-death Jew, begins to rise. Esther is on the move, as she finds favor with the king in her approach and in her first banquet. But that banquet ends with the question of how she will proceed at the next day's banquet. Chapter 5 leaves us hanging, with Haman's gallows rising ominously against the night sky. It's chapter 6 that makes the turn, beginning with a king who could not sleep and ending with a dramatic reversal in the trajectories of these two men. That reversal will continue and accelerate to the book's end.

The Big Picture

Esther's resolve turns into action, as she approaches King Ahasuerus successfully and then hosts her first banquet for the king and Haman, who is being ironically prepared by the narrator for a very steep fall.

> ### Reflection and Discussion

Read the entire text for this week's study, Esther 5–6. Then consider and write your reflections on the following questions, which move through this section of Esther. (For further background, see the *ESV Study Bible*, pages 858–860, or visit esv.org.)

1. Many Are the Plans . . . (Esther 5)

What have we read previously in Esther that makes the scene in 5:1–8 even more full of drama and tension? As you observe Esther here, what descriptive words come to mind? Comment on the details of this dramatic scene that capture your attention.

In what ways might this scene remind us (and/or not remind us!) of heaven's courtroom?

What are the tone and perspective of the narrative in this scene? Why do you think the narrator does not let us in to Esther's thoughts and feelings as the story continues to unfold?

Now observe Haman, in verses 9–14. This is his high point. What details in these verses reveal just what Haman lives for?

How are we readers left after chapter 5? What are our questions? What might we expect to find next in the narrative?

2. The Smallest Providences (Esther 6)

Between Esther's first banquet (ch. 5) and her second banquet (ch. 7), everything changes in that pivotal chapter 6. Read Esther 6:1–5 and comment on every seemingly "random" occurrence you notice in connection with these verses. How do you respond?

We should be sure to enjoy these next verses! As you observe Haman in verses 6–9, what descriptive words come to mind? Do any proverbs come to mind? (Consider, for example, Prov. 16:18; 25:6–7.)

In Esther 6:10–11, what does the narrator *not* tell us—and what is the effect of this brief telling?

The chapter accelerates to the end—and hurries us ahead. Comment on those final words spoken in Haman's house at this hinge point of the story (v. 13), and contrast the directions of rising and falling we have seen so far in Mordecai and Haman.

From chapters 4–6, make a list of the various kinds of coverings, or clothing, you find. (See also 8:15.) How do they mark the progression of the story?

We are given little comment on Mordecai's responses through these scenes. In what ways has his behavior, even in the background, been important to the unfolding of this plot?

With chapter 6, the direction of the story has reversed itself. At this point, stop and summarize the ways in which this book lets us glimpse not only the courage and faithfulness of God's people but at the same time (and concentrated at the center) the hand of an amazing providence[1] at work.

The repeated mention of Mordecai's Jewishness (5:13; 6:10, 13) reminds us of the point of God's providence in this story: it is to protect his people. Recall God's promises in Genesis 12:1–3 and 2 Samuel 7:12–17. What did God promise to do through his chosen people?

Read through the following three sections on *Gospel Glimpses*, *Whole-Bible Connections*, and *Theological Soundings*. Then take time to consider the *Personal Implications* these sections may have for you.

▶ Gospel Glimpses

FAVOR FROM A KING. In this narrative a pattern emerges—the pattern of a suppliant receiving favor (5:2, 8) from a king who could justly sentence the suppliant to death, according to the law. Instead of death this king gives grace, and grace overflowing: King Ahasuerus's promise of up to half of his kingdom means that he is willing to give generously to Esther. All she has to do is ask. And so the King of heaven does for us, when we come to him as suppliants in the name and through the blood of his Son: he gives us not the death we deserve according to the law, but, instead, the gift of life, and life abundant (John 10:10). We cannot press this pattern far: certainly not the specifics of the

69

scene but rather the general contours remind us of God's grace to us as suppliants of the heavenly King.

GOD'S UNFAILING PURPOSES FOR HIS PEOPLE. Haman's wise men and wife expose a potent truth when they say that if Mordecai is of the Jewish people, Haman "will not overcome him but will surely fall before him" (6:13). With these words they acknowledge a transcendent and omnipotent power at work. They do not grasp what it is, although surely they have heard stories of what the God of Israel did for his people in the past, from the crossing of the Red Sea to the driving out of many nations when they settled in the Promised Land and became a great kingdom. The force they are acknowledging is that of God's unfailing redemptive purposes at work through his chosen people. He has covenanted with this people to do great things through them—eternal things—things that come to fruition in the promised Christ (2 Cor. 1:20). Haman's counselors have bumped up against the truth that God's redemptive purposes will not be thwarted.

▶ Whole-Bible Connections

RISING AND FALLING. These chapters begin the rise of Mordecai and the fall of Haman. The Bible repeatedly celebrates the great reversal brought about by God's hand, ultimately through Christ. Hannah's song, for example, overflows with celebration of God's raising up the hungry, the poor, and the needy, but bringing low the rich, the mighty, the "adversaries of the Lord" (see 1 Sam. 2:1–10). The "Magnificat" of Mary the mother of Jesus praises a God who "has brought down the mighty from their thrones and exalted those of humble estate" (see Luke 1:46–55). It was Simeon who told Mary, "this child is appointed for the fall and rising of many in Israel" (Luke 2:34). Christ came down, died, and was raised. Those who believe in him will be raised forever. Those who oppose him and raise themselves up will be brought down. That is the shape of the Bible's—and within it of Esther's—story.

ROBES OF HONOR. Esther assumes her royal robes in this scene to take up the cause of God's people (5:1). Mordecai goes from sackcloth and ashes (4:1) to royal robes (6:8–10; 8:15). Haman the proud boaster wearing the king's signet ring ends up "with his head covered" (6:12). Scripture often uses clothing to shape the story: Joseph, for example, goes from being stripped of his many-colored robe to receiving Pharaoh's signet ring and being clothed in garments of fine linen with a gold chain about his neck (Gen. 37:23; 41:42). At the other end of the Bible come the final pictures of royal clothing: Christ himself "clothed in a robe dipped in blood" . . . "the armies of heaven, arrayed in fine linen" . . . and the Bride of Christ, to whom it has been granted "to clothe herself with fine linen, bright and pure" (Rev. 19:7–8, 13–14).

Theological Soundings

PROVIDENCE. Yes, providence again! The truth of God's sovereign guidance of all things emerges with special impact in this central chapter 6. There is no great miracle, like that of the Red Sea, in this story. There is, at this crucial juncture, simply the fact that the king couldn't sleep. (And then there's the choosing of a book to read . . .) That God should work through such common, ordinary occurrences is most wonderful, for it reminds us of his sovereign redemptive purposes in every common, ordinary occurrence of our lives—whether we see it and name it as his providence or not. Esther's courageous plan of action encases chapter 6, but chapter 6 stands as the book's hinge, a hinge turned by God's providential hand.

THE SIN OF PRIDE. Haman is the epitome of the proud man whom Scripture warns to beware lest he fall: "One's pride will bring him low, but he who is lowly in spirit will obtain honor" (Prov. 29:23). One might call Mordecai "lowly in spirit" by contrast: it appears that he continued to serve the king for years without receiving or demanding a reward for his special service to him. In planning Mordecai's demise, Haman was living out the warning of Proverbs that "whoever digs a pit will fall into it" (26:27). Haman's story vividly illustrates James 4:6: "God opposes the proud, but gives grace to the humble."

Personal Implications

Take time to reflect on the implications of Esther 5–6 for your own life today. Make notes below on the personal implications for your walk with the Lord that you find in the (1) *Gospel Glimpses*, (2) *Whole-Bible Connections*, (3) *Theological Soundings*, and (4) this passage as a whole.

1. Gospel Glimpses

2. Whole-Bible Connections

3. Theological Soundings

----

4. Esther 5–6

> ### As You Finish This Unit . . .

Take a moment now to ask for the Lord's blessing and help as you continue in this study of Esther. Take a moment also to look back through this unit of study, to reflect on a few key things that the Lord may be teaching you—and perhaps to highlight and underline these things to review again in the future.

Definitions

[1] **Providence** – God's good, wise, and all-powerful guidance of all things, by which he supplies our needs and accomplishes his holy will.

Week 10:
Falling and Rising:
Switched and
Speeding to the End

Esther 7–8

The Place of the Passage

Esther's second feast balances on the other side of chapter 6, tracing the switch of trajectories established by that chapter. As Haman falls and the Jews rise, we sense even more vividly the powerful hand of God on his people. Haman's counselors articulate that sense in Esther 6:13, and then immediately we watch those words come true. In light of the Scriptures, of course, it is more than a sense; it is a surety that God's promises to his people will not fail.

The Big Picture

Haman's fall comes with quick inevitability in chapter 7, followed by Mordecai's rise in chapter 8—which brings with it the rise of the Jewish people, who move from mourning the decree of death to joyfully celebrating the reversal effected by a second decree that protects their lives.

> **Reflection and Discussion**

Read through the complete passage for this study, Esther 7–8. Then consider and write your reflections on the following questions, which move through this section of Esther. (For further background, see the *ESV Study Bible*, pages 860–861, or visit esv.org.)

1. A Second Feast and a Falling (Esther 7)

Before looking at chapter 7 specifically, review where we've come in chapters 5–8. Draw a simple diagram or picture of these chapters' overall shape, indicating in some way the changes in direction and position that take place. Don't worry about artistry . . . just have fun!

Chapter 6 leaves us with a sense of inevitability, and yet Esther still must play her crucial part in the action. When the king makes his generous offer to her (for the third time), how does Esther's response evidence great discernment (7:3–4)? What other words do her words echo, and how is this effective? To what does she appeal? Observe everything you can about Esther's plea.

Notice specifically how Esther names the Jewish people in her plea. Trace the various references to the Jews throughout chapters 1–8. Then comment on *God's* way of referring to the Jews in Exodus 3:7–10 and Leviticus 26:11–13.

To grasp the largest reverberations of this scene, jump out of the text a bit further, glimpsing the extent of God's promises in Jeremiah 31:31–33 and 1 Peter 2:9–10. In this larger context, how might we talk about what Esther is doing as she identifies herself with her people (7:3–4)?

Back to the story ... which rushes to the conclusion of chapter 7 with a series of wonderful ironies. What ironic words and events stand out to you as this chapter recounts the final moments of Haman's demise?

2. A Rising and a Saving (Esther 8)

Esther is the human trigger of the action that brings about the fall of Haman and now the rise of Mordecai. To grasp more of the book's symmetry, make as many specific observations as you can about the ways in which chapter 8 mirrors and undoes the action of chapter 3.

Some have argued over whether Mordecai or Esther is the "hero" or central figure of this narrative. Clearly they are both necessary to the story—but how does Esther 8:1–2 make their relationship clear? (Refer also to the shape of chapters 5–8 as considered in the first question.)

At this point Esther knows the problem is not completely solved. How is her second petition (8:3–6) similar to but different from the first (7:3–4)? What does the king's answer reveal about him (8:7–8)?

So, as the only possible solution, a second edict is issued. How do the details of Esther 8:9–14 *dramatically* undo those in 3:12–15? What is the effect here?

Stop to consider the hand of God, not mentioned but again so clearly evident. How is the timing originally indicated by the casting of lots (3:7) crucial in the unfolding story?

A larger question involves the taking of lives, which will be treated in more detail in the final lesson. For now, consider: how might we see a connection between this edict sanctioning the Jews' destruction of their enemies, and God's promise to Abraham in Genesis 12:3?

_____

_____

_____

_____

_____

_____

_____

Finally, write down and comment on that pile-up of joy-words bursting out of Esther 8:15–17. Then consider the chapter's final statement: what might be some of its implications? How might it relate to the final promise of God to Abraham in Genesis 12:3?

_____

_____

_____

_____

_____

_____

_____

Read through the following three sections on *Gospel Glimpses, Whole-Bible Connections*, and *Theological Soundings*. Then take time to consider the *Personal Implications* these sections may have for you.

Gospel Glimpses

A PLEADING INTERCESSOR. Again not in the details but in the contours of the narrative, the shape of the gospel emerges as an advocate pleading on behalf of a people that they might be saved from destruction. In these chapters we see the intercessor actually doing the pleading: Esther here represents her people before a sovereign king. He is a poor figure of a king (pointing only by contrast to the heavenly one), but in King Ahasuerus's hand rests the fate of God's people for whom Esther pleads. And again, no figure points more than blurrily and inadequately to the righteous Son of God who intercedes for us. All such earthly dramas remind us of the one great heavenly one, in which Christ Jesus represents his people before a holy God, whose wrath is turned away by the atonement made by Christ himself on the cross (1 John 2:1–2).

AT THE RIGHT TIME. The Bible makes clear that salvation happened according to God's plan, with Christ our Savior coming and dying for us "at the right time" (Rom. 5:6), "when the fullness of time had come" (Gal. 4:4). The sovereign timing of the salvation story in Esther shows the ways of this same God, who determines the outcome of the casting of lots in 3:7, thereby allowing the perfect time span for not just one but two separate decrees to be sent out from Susa to the far ends of the Persian empire. Even the timing of Haman's entrance into the court in chapter 6 is clearly ordained—and all not just for a good story but for the story of God's people being saved from death. We glimpse here a sovereign God who at the right time perfectly saves his people.

A GOSPEL FOR THE NATIONS. When we read in Esther 8:17 that many among the peoples of the Persian empire declared themselves Jews, for fear of the Jews, we cannot help but think of God's promise that through Abraham's seed all the peoples of the earth will be blessed (Gen. 12:3). Of course much of the "fear" in Esther's time might be plain old unrepentant fright, as with the Canaanites whose "hearts melted" when they heard what God had done for his people (Josh. 2:11). But that report in Joshua came from the mouth of the Canaanite Rahab, who heard and whose heart both melted and believed. God was drawing the nations with his saving truth, just as he promised. There may have been some Rahabs throughout the Persian empire, drawn perhaps not only by proper fear of such a God but also by the gladness and joy of his people, as the Spirit savingly melted their hearts.

Whole-Bible Connections

REJOICING OF GOD'S PEOPLE. Certainly not all the Jews who rejoiced at being saved were Jews who faithfully followed God. But what we see here are God's people rejoicing at being saved (and their enemies destroyed). Such rejoicing resounds throughout Scripture, from the victory song sung after the exodus (Exodus 15), to the rejoicing over the defeat of Moab and Sihon and Og (Numbers 21), to Deborah's song after the defeat of the Canaanites (Judges 5), and so on. But even in the Old Testament the rejoicing of God's people points to more than temporal battles; it points to an eternal God who rules all the nations with perfect justice and who blesses all who take refuge in him—

ultimately through his Son (Psalm 2). In Jesus Christ, the promised Seed of Abraham, is the full and final rejoicing of all God's people. Such feasting and rejoicing as we see in Esther only dimly foreshadows the eternal rejoicing we shall know in heaven with our risen and conquering Lamb (Rev. 19:1–16).

LIFE AND DEATH. Esther 7–8 is about who will live and who will die. From the beginning there have been the two great and opposite realities: in the garden of Eden stood the tree of life, and the man and woman ate from the forbidden tree and were condemned to death. The Bible is all about God conquering death on our behalf to give us new life. God promised and brought about that new life through the people we watch in the Old Testament—the Jews. From them came the promised Christ, who died to bring life to all God's people from all the nations. The only alternative to this life is death. Esther offers a vivid glimpse into the life-and-death ramifications of God's redemptive plan promised through the Jewish people. To reject this people and their God was to align with death, ultimately in opposition to God's redemptive plan. Esther, in saving her people, is aligning herself with life—with God's redemptive plan through his chosen people.

Theological Soundings

GOD'S PEOPLE. When Esther finally names her people, calling them "my people," she aligns herself with the ones to whom and through whom God has promised blessing (Gen. 12:1–3). She is standing with and in God's covenant community, as part of the people receiving his promises. The "Reflection and Discussion" questions pointed us to passages that show the extent of those promises (Lev. 26:11–13; Jer. 31:31–33; 1 Pet. 2:9–10)—all finally fulfilled in Jesus Christ, who came to die for us and make us his, a people for his own possession, his very body. Faith in the Lord God has never been only an individual matter; it means becoming part of God's people, joining a blessed and blessing community of those living out the promises of God in Christ. We do not know if Esther's heart was a heart of faith. What we can see is that she (and Mordecai) stood in the place of blessing, with God's covenant people.

A SOVEREIGN KING. King Ahasuerus continues to offer perverse but telling hints of divine sovereignty. We glimpse here a king's power to bestow untold royal riches (7:2; 8:1–2); the force of a king's wrath that condemns a man to death on the spot (7:10); the terror of facing such wrath (7:6); and the need for favor from such a sovereign, who holds nations in his hands (7:3; 8:5). Esther 3:8–11 and 8:7–8 show how little *this* king cares about the lives of his subjects; such glimpses make us eternally glad for a heavenly King who is this powerful and far more—but who shows grace and mercy to those he rules, making a way for them to know him and to share his glory forever, through his own Son.

Personal Implications

Take time to reflect on the implications of Esther 7–8 for your own life today. Make notes below on the personal implications for your walk with the Lord that you find in the (1) *Gospel Glimpses*, (2) *Whole-Bible Connections*, (3) *Theological Soundings*, and (4) this passage as a whole.

1. Gospel Glimpses

2. Whole-Bible Connections

3. Theological Soundings

4. Esther 7–8

As You Finish This Unit . . .

Take a moment now to ask for the Lord's blessing and help as you continue in this study of Esther. Take a moment also to look back through this unit of study, to reflect on a few key things that the Lord may be teaching you—and perhaps to highlight and underline these things to review again in the future.

WEEK 11: REVERSAL: CONSUMMATED, CELEBRATED, AND CONCLUDED

Esther 9–10

▲

By the time we reach the final two chapters of Esther, the plot has been resolved. Esther 9–10 offers us what in literature is called the denouement, or the unraveling of all the pieces that have been put finally in place. Similarly, in the overarching biblical storyline of redemption, after the climax of the cross and the resurrection, what remains is to reap the fruit of that climax as we move toward the story's consummation, its final piece. The consummation of Esther, like that of redemption's story, involves not only the life of God's people but the death of their enemies. The book ends with Queen Esther in a position of authority, having seen to the utter downfall of Haman's house and influence, and the high honor of Mordecai, who uses his power for the welfare of the Jewish people.

The Big Picture

Esther 9–10 tells of the Jews' victory over their enemies and their celebratory feasting on the fourteenth and fifteenth days of Adar, establishing those dates as the documented source of the Jewish Feast of Purim. Esther and Mordecai are firmly established as powerful rulers under King Ahasuerus, seeking the good of their people, the Jews.

Reflection and Discussion

Read through Esther 9–10, the passage for this week's study. Then consider and write your reflections on the following questions, which move through this final section of Esther. (For further background, see the *ESV Study Bible*, pages 861–863, or visit esv.org.)

1. The Reversal Consummated (Esther 9:1–16)

In many ways, Esther 8:15–17 might have been a nice conclusion to the book. The final chapters, however, bring home the full implications of that conclusion—first by summarizing the final shape of the action. Summarize the grand summary in Esther 9:1! How do the first four verses of chapter 9 dramatically reveal the reversal that has occurred?

Let us recall the larger scriptural context of the battles sanctioned by God in which his people were to destroy whole ungodly cities or nations and take nothing for themselves, devoting everything to destruction as a kind of offering to the Lord. The total destruction of Jericho, for example (except for Rahab and her family) was clearly commanded and carried out (Josh. 6:15–25). Achan disobeyed the command of destruction at Ai, with deadly results (Joshua 7). Now, having recalled this background, review 1 Samuel 15: in what ways did

Mordecai's ancestor Saul fail in that story? In what ways might Esther 9:5–16 seem to bring final resolution to that story?

We have returned many times to the background of God's covenant with Abraham in Genesis 12:1–3 and his covenant with David in 2 Samuel 7:12–17. How does the background of both the covenants and the battles help us see our Lord God more clearly? How does all this background help illumine the final battles of Esther?

What about God's people *now*? The promised Christ has come, through the seed of Abraham and in the line of David; he has accomplished our salvation on the cross and in his resurrection from the dead. Through faith in him we are the spiritual descendants of Abraham (Gal. 3:29). We his people no longer fight physical battles as a physical nation. According to Ephesians 6:10–12, what kinds of battles do we fight now, as God's people in Christ?

Even though the climax of our salvation story has been accomplished in Christ's first coming, our story awaits the consummation, just as Esther's story awaited that set day of battle. Write down several things 2 Thessalonians 1:5–10 reveals about the day of Christ's second coming.[1] How might these words of Paul help us see what Esther 9:5–16 is showing us about God?

What should be our response to the huge reality of God's wrath and eternal punishment coming for those who have not by faith in Christ become part of God's people?

2. The Reversal Celebrated (Esther 9:17–32)

The feasting and gladness come in the text soon after the battles and destruction (as in Moses' song in Exodus 15, and many other passages). Look ahead to the promised final feast, the marriage supper of the Lamb, in Revelation 19:6–9—and glance through the larger context of that whole chapter. Write your observations.

Esther 9:17–18 tells of two closing feasts. Recall the two opening feasts (1:4–5). Esther's two feasts are in the middle. What might you observe about these feasts and their relation to the book's themes and structure?

Summarize the explanation for the Feast of Purim (Esther 9:20–27). Review Hannah's song in 1 Samuel 2:1–10 and Mary's song in Luke 1:46–55. What similar themes do you notice?

Notice the repeated emphasis on writing all this down, in Esther 9:20–32. Why this emphasis, do you think?

3. The Reversal Concluded (Esther 10:1–3)

Note and comment on the various ways in which Mordecai is shown to be raised up high in these final verses.

What phrases call attention to the Jews in the final verses? Many have found here echoes of Psalm 122:6–9. What connections do you see?

There is great resolution in Esther 10—but is there also an implicit longing? With what degree of closure does this book end?

Read through the following three sections on *Gospel Glimpses*, *Whole-Bible Connections*, and *Theological Soundings*. Then take time to consider the *Personal Implications* these sections may have for you.

Gospel Glimpses

SAVED FROM GOD'S WRATH.[2] In the final victory of Esther we see a vivid portrayal both of God's steadfast love for his people and of God's holy wrath that punishes his enemies. This is a hard whole truth. But surely it is the truth pictured large for us throughout the Old Testament and taught fully in the New Testament—so that we will turn to this God and repent, and he will have mercy on us, only and ultimately through the blood of Christ. At the cross shine forth both God's justice and God's mercy. His mercy is more beautiful in our eyes when we understand that, without it, we are all "dead" in our sin and "children of wrath" (Eph. 2:1–3).

THE GREAT REVERSAL. Esther's final chapters show the book's reversal brought to its logical and emphatic conclusion. Not only is Haman dead, but so are all his sons. Not only are those sons dead; they are hanged publicly, for all to see. Not only is there one day of killing in Susa; there's also another. Mordecai, whose rising has matched Haman's falling, exits not just with honor but with "high honor," "advanced" by the king, "second in rank to King Ahasuerus," "great among the Jews." We're meant to feel the full weight of the reversal that has occurred. The gospel itself shows the most amazing reversal: how can we ever feel the full weight of the fact that the Son of God descended to the depths of death on a cross, so that we his people might be raised to unimaginable and eternal rejoicing in his very presence?

Whole-Bible Connections

DEVOTING TO DESTRUCTION. In the description of the Jews' victory comes the repeated insistence that *they laid no hands on the plunder* (9:10, 15, 16). This is all the more remarkable as the second edict permitted them to "destroy, to kill, and to annihilate" their enemies *and to plunder their goods* (8:11), which of course exactly mirrored the original edict (3:13). This one huge disconnect stands out—and connects us to the biblical records of those battles in which God commissioned his people to devote everything in a pagan city to complete destruction, keeping nothing for themselves. Mordecai's ancestor Saul disobeyed this command in regard to the Amalekites, their King Agag, and their cattle (1 Samuel 15); when Mordecai and his people obey this command in regard to Haman the Agagite and those who follow him, they are in a sense resolving a whole history of divinely commissioned warfare.

FEASTING. Esther abounds with feasting. Feasts not only structure the book; they also connect with a broader biblical theme of the joyful communion of God's redeemed people. It is important that we be shown the pagan feasts on the front end of Esther being replaced finally with the feasting of God's people: this is the movement of the book. Esther's feasts in the center provide the transitional links, in which life and joy are being transferred from God's enemies to his people. The Bible offers many pictures of the feasting-fellowship of God's redeemed people: from the Passover Feast (of which this story's calendar references remind us) . . . to the Lord's Supper instituted in the New Testament . . . to the marriage supper of the Lamb in Revelation. The feasts in Esther resonate with this larger biblical theme.

Theological Soundings

GOD'S UNFAILING WORD. We affirmed that the story has been resolved by the time we reach these last two chapters. Truly it was resolved long before— certainly as far back as God's eternal redemptive purposes revealed in his promises to this chosen people: that through their seed he would bring blessing to all the nations of the world, and that from David's line would come a king who would rule the nations perfectly and forever. This story shows the unfailing truth of those covenant promises to this people. God's redemptive purposes are at work, according to his word. There is no direct word from God within the story of Esther. But his promises from the biblical context surround and echo, proving true even when not acknowledged or spoken.

KINGSHIP; GOD'S PERFECT RULE. Chapter 10 shows Mordecai to be a good ruler, seeking his people's welfare. But before him and above him these final words point to King Ahasuerus, the one with power and might—and, we know, one who is not good like Mordecai, not really caring about the welfare of God's people but mainly about his own. When we close with the beautiful assertion that Mordecai "sought the welfare of his people and spoke peace to all his people," we do tend to hear echoes of psalms or prophecies in which such a leader acts and speaks. God's people at this point in history have lost their kingdom and their king. But they have been promised a king who will come and reign forever. The longing for that good King may lurk in these ringing last words of Esther.

Personal Implications

Take time to reflect on the implications of Esther 9–10 for your own life today. Make notes below on the personal implications for your walk with the Lord that you find in the (1) *Gospel Glimpses*, (2) *Whole-Bible Connections*, (3) *Theological Soundings*, and (4) this passage as a whole.

1. Gospel Glimpses

2. Whole-Bible Connections

3. Theological Soundings

4. Esther 9–10

▶ As You Finish This Unit . . .

Take a moment now to ask for the Lord's blessing and help as you prepare to conclude this study of Esther and Ruth. Take a moment also to look back through this unit of study, to reflect on a few key things the Lord may be teaching you—and perhaps to highlight and underline these things to review again in the future.

Definitions

[1] **Second coming of Christ** – Jesus came two thousand years ago for the first time. One day he will return to earth again, this time not in disguise but openly as the ruler of all (Rev. 19:11–21).

[2] **Wrath** – God's righteous and just anger over human rebellion. Jesus exhausted God's wrath on the cross for all who trust in him.

Week 12: Summary and Conclusion

▲

We will conclude our study of Ruth and Esther by summarizing the big picture of God's message in these two narratives. We will then reflect on various Gospel Glimpses, Whole-Bible Connections, and Theological Soundings throughout Ruth and Esther.

The Big Picture of Ruth and Esther

Both Ruth and Esther tell a story of the God who blesses his people according to his promises. In both books the prospect of those promises at first looks dark. In Ruth, the darkness comes not only from the personal desolation of Naomi's family but also from the context of the period of the judges, when Israel did not follow God. In Esther, the darkness comes from the pagan setting of the Persian court after the exile, from the threatened annihilation of the Jewish race, and from the fact that God is never mentioned in the course of the narrative.

In each of these narratives, God's promises prevail not only through the courage of a remarkable woman but, even more, through the merciful providence of the Lord God. As Ruth the Moabitess walks by faith into Bethlehem with her bitter mother-in-law Naomi, scene by scene we glimpse the loving kindness of

God's promised provision pouring into Ruth's family, into God's people, and into all the nations of the world—ultimately through Jesus.

God's provision is not overt in Esther as it is in Ruth. We are far from the Promised Land, in the palaces of Susa. The surface action is glittering with gold but dark with the absence of God's name. The narrative of Esther offers us not a plain unfolding of scenes but an intricate series of patterns and reversals that point to themselves and ask us to find their meaning. In the very shape of the narrative emerge the raising up of God's people and the destruction of his enemies that together show God's promises in action.

Over both stories looms a king. In Ruth, it's King David to come. In Esther, King David's kingdom has come and gone, and the only king in sight is a selfish Persian despot. Both stories are about trusting God's promises in the dark, finding the patterns of his providence that lead to the ultimate provision of light and joy through an eternal king—King Jesus.

Neither of these narratives tells of grand miracles. Each in its own context tells of God's providence at work in the imperfect lives of his called-out people—with huge historical and redemptive ramifications. Ruth and Esther both let us glimpse God's redemptive hand in human history, unfolding his plan to bring blessing to the world through Abraham's seed.

Gospel Glimpses

Both Ruth and Esther show the unfolding of God's redemptive plan, at two different points in Old Testament history. Each story focuses on the significance of God's *people*, this seed through whom God promised blessing—and through whom the promised Redeemer would come. In Ruth we see God in his loving kindness providing for his people even in the midst of rebellion against him, giving them refuge under his wings, redeeming them in love that points us to the love of Christ. In Esther we see the wonder of the ways of God, a God who watches over his people, who makes a way for them to prosper, whose enemies will fall—and who will accomplish his purposes to raise up a people for himself through the perfect promised King.

Mention a few of the ways each of these books helps you see the scope and beauty of God's redemptive plan that culminated in Christ's coming.

List several attributes of God that have emerged in these stories, aspects of his nature on which our salvation depends. Point to a passage or two to explain what you've seen.

How have these books helped you glimpse the gospel not only as a personal, individual matter, but also as God creating a people, in fact, from all the peoples of the world?

Whole-Bible Connections

Both Ruth and Esther connect with biblical themes from the beginning of the Bible to the end—from battles in the Pentateuch to marriage suppers in Revelation. The Bible has one overarching storyline, and every little story connects to the big one: that is, everything connects to the big theme of God redeeming a people for himself through Christ. Boaz is first a redeemer in that he marries Ruth and saves her family's inheritance—but Boaz must point us to Christ our Redeemer, who pays the price for our redemption and provides for us a priceless inheritance. Esther is first a queen who risks her life to beg for mercy from the king—but she connects with many types of intercessors who plead on behalf of their people: we might think of Moses, and we surely think of Christ and the perfect plea of his blood on our behalf before the throne of God.

Has your understanding of the unity of the Bible been clarified through studying Ruth and Esther? How so?

Comment on several of the whole-Bible themes in Ruth and Esther that stood out to you or that you hadn't noticed before.

In what ways has this study filled out your understanding of the biblical story-line of redemption?

Theological Soundings

Ruth and Esther have much to contribute to Christian theology, not through direct teaching but through narrative that tells the truth about God's nature and his redemptive plan. Some of the theological truths that emerge from these stories relate to sovereignty; providence; grace; grace, faith, and works; the kingdom of God; God's unfailing word; God's judgment of sin; worship/idolatry; the inheritance of faith; and marriage and sexual purity as they reflect God.

Where has your theology been adjusted or developed as you have studied Ruth and Esther? Explain.

How has your understanding of the nature and character of God been deepened throughout this study?

What unique contributions do Ruth and/or Esther make toward our understanding of Jesus?

What, specifically, do Ruth and/or Esther teach us about the human condition?

Personal Implications

Finally, as you reflect on Ruth and Esther, what implications do you see for your own life? For example, how might your study of these books affect your prayers, your trust in God's promises, your love for his Word, your heart for evangelism . . . ? Write your concluding thoughts.

As You Finish Studying Ruth and Esther . . .

We rejoice with you as you finish studying the books of Ruth and Esther! May this study become part of your Christian walk of faith, day by day and week by week throughout all your life. Now we would greatly encourage you to continue to study the Word of God on a week-by-week basis. To continue your study of the Bible, we would encourage you to consider other books in the Knowing the Bible series, and to visit www.knowingthebibleseries.org.

Lastly, take a moment again to look back through Ruth and Esther, which you have studied during these recent weeks. Review again the notes that you have written, and the things that you have highlighted or underlined. Reflect again on the key themes that the Lord has been teaching you about himself and about his Word. May these things become a treasure for you throughout your life—which we pray will be true for you, in the name of the Father, and the Son, and the Holy Spirit. Amen.